STRAVINSKY

A New Appraisal of His Work

PAUL HENRY LANG was born in Budapest in 1901. After studying at Heidelberg and the Sorbonne, he came to the United States in 1928 and received his Ph.D. degree from Cornell in 1934. Since 1939 he has been professor of musicology at Columbia University, since 1945 editor of *The Musical Quarterly,* and since 1954 music critic of the New York *Herald Tribune.* He is the author of *Music in Western Civilization* (1941).

STRAVINSKY

A New Appraisal of His Work

Edited by PAUL HENRY LANG

With a Complete List of Works

The Norton Library
W · W · NORTON & COMPANY · INC ·
NEW YORK

CONTENTS

INTRODUCTION

By PAUL HENRY LANG

THERE are a few powerful figures in whom the main strands of music history seem to knot themselves before diverging again to form a new pattern. Igor Stravinsky, whose eightieth birthday we are celebrating, is a knot — and a mighty hard one — of this kind. Right now Mr. Stravinsky is all the mode. His early works, after the customary time lag of some forty or fifty years, are well liked by the public, his latest, the dodecaphonic, vastly admired by the progressive professionals. But the aging master has demonstrated that it is possible for the modish to retain their individuality, for he has retained his.

Such a long and distinguished career, punctuated by the most unexpected and exciting tangential departures from the norm, was bound to evoke criticisms that run the gamut from one extreme to the other, yet neither those who see in the great Russian composer the deliverer of latter-day music, nor those who regard him a composer of "nihilistic motor music" are right. What Mr. Stravinsky sought above all throughout his many metamorphoses of style was an opportunity and frame for the exercising of a powerful musical instinct, ever alert, original, always seeking new outlets. He did not want to deliver but to conquer, he did not want nihilism but a most exquisitely *raffiné* game in which he created an idiom that is irreducibly his own, an idiom that for half a century has fascinated friend and foe alike, and without which the music of our century would have taken an altogether different turn. His major works stand, amidst the clay of much current music, like rocks flung up from some buried granitic stratum, often disturbing but always undeniable. The reader will remember that Michelangelo used to say he saw the statue inside the block of marble and he merely removed with his chisel the chips that were hiding it from the rest of the world. In a sense, Mr. Stravinsky has the same kind of mind. He sees his music in a clear perspective, with all its

combinations and details and subsidiary operations, and he sees it in
its actual proportions, that is to say, with his mental vision entirely
unclouded by the mass of minor compositional business. His is the
extreme lucidity of one who is completely master of his subject.

It is hard at present to realize how great has been the increase,
during the last half century, in the knowledge of music and its history;
but the effort to envisage the change does at least help us to see contemporary art in more correct proportions and perspective, and to
estimate its trends, its sources, and its failures with greater assurance. The
time is rife for a new study of Igor Stravinsky in the light of modern
sympathies. He is already remote enough for us to have some inkling of
what the future will make of him. The essays in this volume (originally
written for a special issue of *The Musical Quarterly*) have indeed a
subject well worth studying and the study has been well done. While
it is impossible within the space of a small book to do more than touch
upon certain aspects of a major composer's art, perhaps these articles will
do away with the quality of somnambulism that characterizes the manner
in which writers have often approached the problems raised by Mr.
Stravinsky's art. We must interpret him from the angle of his particular
historic cultural position, which is almost a mission. The following articles
do this most brilliantly, and what the Editor is about to say is without
prejudice to the able writers' assessment of Igor Stravinsky's creations;
we merely want to make some observations that will perhaps complement
their findings.

*   *

*

The farther one gets into Mr. Stravinsky's life work the more cause
one finds for admiration of the composer's skill, invention, and fluency.
At the same time, however, one looks in vain for some sort of vision,
some gift of poetry or revelation that would invest his *oeuvre* with a
significance denied to lesser composers. A certain transmitting power
is absent beginning with his middle period; in these admirably crafted
compositions there are no more heights to scale from adventure to
adventure. It appears that the strengths and weaknesses of his music,
once he had abandoned his Russian heritage and turned altogether
to the West, are due to the close pondering he gives to it. Even when
he is wondrously lyrical — which is very rare — as in the *Symphony
of Psalms,* he sings with a certain planned precision. In more recent
times, however, he is likely to lapse from a happy precision into an
elegantly quaint pedantry. Form and mindfulness always remain most

sensitively fused, but the lack of feeling reflects the sterilities of the scientific age that is upon us. What is unsatisfactory in these molded and polished works is the want of something that is best described as introspection.

What is introspection? The question is necessary because very different activities are included under the term. A good example of a definition is to be found in a paragraph in Coleridge's *Anima Poetae:* "Now let me think of *myself* — of the thinking being. The idea becomes dim, whatever it be — so dim that I know not what it is; but the feeling is deep and steady, and this I can call *I* — identifying the percipient and the perceived." This identification, it seems, is largely absent in Mr. Stravinsky's music; it is always brilliant and magnificently tooled, and at his best he achieves dignity and resonance, but seldom real intimacy; there is almost always a greater interest in impeccable style and manner than in message. Indeed, what Saint-Saëns said jokingly about *Tristan* at times applies with uncomfortable validity to Mr. Stravinsky's works: *Un spectacle dans un fauteuil avec orchestre.* It stands to reason, of course, that a composer's nature is not to be sought in his feelings alone, but in his thought and will, despite the fact that many seem to object to intellect and will in art — it would be equally logical to treat architecture as a minor branch of building. But the "anti-intellectualist" has an important point in his favor even though he is seldom entirely clear about it. There are persons so enamored of learning, of the pure and abstract manipulation of substance, that they disregard — even dismiss, as Mr. Stravinsky has done — all other capabilities of the soul. Mere intellect, learning and skill alone, would simply and inexorably divest man of his personality, he would become a mere quantum. As physics triumphs over nature by viewing it as an aggregation of atoms to which it can apply mathematics — that great creation of the human mind — so the mind of the abstract intellectualist views the human atoms, of which music is one, as so many elements that can be apprehended and exposed in cold figures and convolutions. In this music no meaning is possible for the "mind" to review, or for the "spirit" to kindle at, till the "brain" has mastered the musico-geometric relationship. This concept of music is mechanical-scientific, its structure is supposed to be as intelligble as that of a piece of machinery to the engineer who built it; no esthetic-ethical problem is involved. Idealism is a myth and the tradition of musical culture is a mere burden on intelligence, a dodge to maintain the status quo though circumstances change. Regard for tradition is therefore seen as a form of mental decay.

The twelve-tone "system" looks back upon a generation of continually increasing activity, which began with the impact of Schoenberg on international musical thought. More recently knowledge of "the art of composing with twelve tones" became the road to possession of truly contemporary style and thought. The difficult and disciplined language of Schoenberg has been mastered not only by Austrians and Germans, but by Italians, Frenchmen, Englishmen, Americans — and Mr. Stravinsky — on a scale and with a fanatic intensity to which the world can show few parallels. Nevertheless, this achievement exacted its price by absorbing far too much of the musicians' mental energy. At that, in most cases the influence was accepted rather than absorbed, and the influence rarely went to the center, where imagination is touched and awakened. The necessity of working in a medium that every moment requires attention to itself has laid heavy burdens on the mind. Yet, when taking stock after a third of a century of music influenced by serial principles, we find ourselves observing with astonished admiration that in quite a few musicians creative imagination has overcome the disabilities, and their music has taken in not only the formal but the essential. Dodecaphonic music has been — and is — often deplorable, commentaries upon it have been bewilderingly dark. Students have been presented with categories that have been meaningless to most of them, for in the absence of a properly elaborated esthetic concept their teachers are constrained to treat the subject as a mechanical art with arbitrary rules. Yet genius has repeatedly avoided the shoals or minimized their presence.

As is well known, Mr. Stravinsky's latest stylistic reorientation brought him within the serial camp. There is a great swagger about this conversion which the partisans celebrate in the musical equivalent of the "from log cabin to the White House" motif, an excellent motif for romance. The strange but profoundly original creative mind of Mr. Stravinsky is as sure in the serial orbit as he is essentially not of it. Like all converts he is emphatic about declaring his allegiance to "the three Viennese," and his apologists insist on some plausible but disingenuous plea of necessity which seems to be corroborated by Mr. Stravinsky's gradual rapprochement to a style he once ignored if not despised. Did not Debussy predict as early as 1917 that the Russian master would end in Schoenberg's retinue? In a letter to Robert Godet, Debussy made this astonishingly clairvoyant statement: "In my opinion the young Russian school has become as little Russian as possible. Stravinsky himself inclines dangerously towards the side of Schoenberg, nevertheless he remains the most marvelous orchestral mechanic of these times." Edward T. Cone, in his very perceptive article, shows how the Stravinsky mind operates in this medium with the same assuredness and powerful logic we find in all his styles; still, dodecaphony is no more his real domain than was neo-Classicism, and this despite several unquestionable masterpieces. But before we take up the stations of this rapprochement we must deal with the reasons for the stations themselves, with the celebrated case of the "1001 styles."

In his autobiography, Carl Philipp Emanuel Bach analyzes the reasons for his own stylistic peregrinations in this interesting paragraph.

> It is because I have never liked excessive uniformity in composition or taste, because I have heard many different kinds of good things, because it has always been my opinion that the good should be accepted regardless of where it may be found, even when it appears in small details of a piece; it is because of these considerations and the assistance of a God-given natural ability that the variety which is attributed to my compositions has arisen.

This is an astonishingly good description of Mr. Stravinsky's own musical *curriculum vitae,* and it accords so well with views expressed by him that one would think that truth has seldom been so aptly demonstrated. If we look at the scores absolutely, as works of the musical imagination independent of time and place and free from all limitations set by the knowledge and prejudices of the outside world, we may find this parallel. But that would mean sweeping aside the evidence of life, for we must also know the scores as conditioned by time and place and material needs and physical means of expression. To be thus never quite at home is to be always on the watch for the different. At times the difference, though always based on careful observation, strikes us in Mr. Stravinsky's case as being calculated, whereas Emanuel Bach was usually probing, happily embarking upon an adventure the outcome of which he only sensed. As a consequence his catalogue of works shows genuine masterpieces next to essays in experiment. Mr. Stravinsky always knows exactly what he is doing, what he wants, whither he is going, and what he will attain.

The interpreter of a creative genius must find the center from which the organization of the inner man takes its departure. With less complicated personalities than Mr. Stravinsky these traits are more easily apprehended, but with the aid of the interesting criticisms made by his erstwhile compatriots, so ably selected and complemented by Professor Schwarz, and leaning on Mr. Mellers's acute asides as well as Mr. Morton's clever and revealing detective work, we may come to some conclusions. It goes without saying that whatever our honored Russian colleagues say must be rubbed with alcohol, bleached, and dehydrated of dialecticism and Social Realism before their statements can be admitted to the record. However, Professor Schwarz was not fooled by the verbiage and managed to find not only the approved but also the suppressed documents, and one can also read between and behind the lines. There is no question that beneath the camouflage there is a good deal of truth; the Russians divined Mr. Stravinsky's true nature, for he is after all one of their own.

Today, and contrary to Mr. Stravinsky's own protestations, it is clear that the impulses that animated the great composer's most original and productive period, from *L'Oiseau de feu* to *Les Noces,* came from Russian music, both popular and the Rimsky-dominated Westernized national school. All we have to do is to recall the Princess's scene in *L'Oiseau de feu,* the scene at the fair in *Petrushka,* the Russian dance or the *Rondes printanières* in *Le Sacre* — all this is inexorably connected with Russian music. Mr. Stravinsky, an instinctively secure stage composer, always knows what to select from this folk music: the illustrative, spectacularly active and dynamic elements which at the same time lend themselves to closed formal treatment. Such an artist does not grasp in folk music what is most profound, as did Mussorgsky and Bartók; on the other hand, whatever he borrows will become more colorful, interesting, and dazzling in his hands. The qualities that make this possible were present in Mr. Stravinsky in profusion and eventually made him the most admired and fashionable modern composer, though by the time this admiration became general he was no longer a Russian composer but a Westerner *par excellence,* worshipped by the youth of Western Europe as their leader and practically ignored by his former countrymen. After *Petrushka* he severed himself from his country not only physically, but by stages also spiritually, though occasional Russian themes appear in later works. He was now a great international artist whose base of operations was French culture. Already in *Rossignol* Debussy's influence is unmistakable, and by the time of the first World War the French began to consider him a Frenchman by inclination and taste. There can be no question that in *Le Sacre* Mr. Stravinsky was closest to the aspirations of his youth; even though he now rejects critical opinions that see in this a powerful apotheosis of elemental passions, primeval man, and the cosmic forces of nature. Nor can there be any doubt that in the marvelous imagination of this work, in its orgiastic, evocative accents, achieved by new and original means, with its extraordinary pictorial, dynamic, and kinetic scale of expressivity, he conjured up the wild vision of a primordial Asian folk rite.

"Rite" is not only a title. Mr. Mellers comes to the conclusion that for Stravinsky "music has always been ritual." Very true. There is, however, a tremendous difference between a ritual such as *Le Sacre,* which is a blazing experience, and the Mass and *Canticum sacrum,* which are formal thought and dogma. Professor Schwarz quotes Asafiev, the Soviet critic, who clearly saw Stravinsky's deep roots in Russia and Russian music, who found his neo-Classic reincarnation as "Europeanization of Stravinsky's musical language"; indeed, he called the idiom a sort of musical Esperanto. Asafiev is highly laudatory about the "Russian" Stravinsky, welcoming his boldness and power, but this was said before the clammy hand of official party esthetics choked the critic's voice. Even in later Soviet writings, under the childish petulance, the faithful echoing of the party line, and even the more coarse and vicious invectives of the zealots such as the unsavory Khrennikov, there is a palpable regret at having lost a Russian composer who had foresworn his patrimony and turned against the land that bore and nourished him. And there is a good deal of evidence to show that at bottom this feeling was reciprocated, that the cosmopolitan exterior of Mr. Stravinsky hides the *deraciné* eternally longing for the lost soil. This is Mr. Stravinsky's tragedy, which explains the restless search that followed after *Les Noces,* the last Russian "ritual." He could always find new and exciting tones and accents, but he could not find a genuine haven. In this connection there is significance in what Lawrence Morton found out about Mr. Stravinsky's Russian sympathies long after the last moorings were cast away. Mr. Morton points out that Stravinsky's admiration for Tchaikovsky "remained an article of musical faith" throughout his life, and "that charming *opera buffa, Mavra,* celebrated the three Russian artists he most admired: Pushkin, Glinka, and Tchaikovsky." As late as 1928, *Le Baiser de la fée* was dedicated to the memory of Tchaikovsky and utilized various tunes borrowed from the older composer. Mr. Morton's analysis of the work is striking: he contends that *Le Baiser* is both homage and criticism, nevertheless he too feels that "at a certain moment of his career Stravinsky needed the figure of Tchaikovsky as a symbol of Russian music from which he himself stemmed."

With *Le Sacre* Mr. Stravinsky inaugurated an activist-dynamic-barbaric tendency in the heartland of hedonistic Impressionism that stunned Western Europe, and he became the recognized leader of the movement. But while his admirers desperately tried to follow him, after a few lighter and more sophisticated virtuoso episodes he suddenly took a totally different tack. In the first decade of his professional life the Russian composer was interested mainly in the stage, then he turned to chamber music, sonata, and concerto, though this period also saw two important stage works, *Oedipus Rex* and *Apollon Musagète*. It is amusing to record what Mr. Stravinsky said to Alfredo Casella after playing for him the *Eight Easy Pieces for Piano Four Hands:* neo-Classicism "was born in that moment." Not so amusing is what he said concerning the Sonata for piano, the Concerto for piano and wind instruments, and especially the Octet for winds. Here he endeavored "to establish order and discipline in the purely sonorous scheme to which I always give precedence over elements of an emotional character." Such words and such ideas were never known on the banks of the Volga — Russia had been abandoned forever. All the elements that had hitherto appeared in his works as formal factors, the "motor" drive, the motif repetitions, dynamic piling up rather than development, the love of insistent rhythms, the raw presentation of primitive materials in the center of a sophisticated texture (Debussy on *Le Sacre:* "Savage music with all modern conveniences"), now were replaced by jazz, or by such exotic excursions as the Japanese songs, finally finding a seemingly natural home in the forms of 18th-century Classicism, concerto, divertimento, *opera buffa*. He could not of course really assimilate and express the original content of these forms, but being a many-sided artist who dreads stagnation, he welcomed and enjoyed them as decorative frames and played with them — perhaps because with their aid he could avoid the real problems. As a born dramatic composer he shaped the *chef d'oeuvre* of the neo-Classic phase for the stage: *Oedipus Rex,* the Greco-Latin scenic oratorio by way of — Cocteau, whose French text had to be translated into Latin. Here is neo-Classicism with a vengeance! The dramatic lines of this music, though deliberately marmoreal, are unfolded with a sure and unencumbered freedom, the choruses, the decorative background, monodic recitation, the *testo,* the whole arsenal of Baroque dramatic music is magnificently blended; what is missing is the weight of inner artistic necessity which makes great creations believable. *Oedipus Rex* is the wonderful handiwork of a full-blooded musician, but there is more cool observation and reflection in this, as well as in other compositions of the neo-Classic period, than compelling experience. The artificial Latin evoked artificial gestures. Yet Mr. Stravinsky's conceits cling close to the logic of music and his very self-possession enables him to handle the oddest subjects and materials more distinctively than many of those who approach music through passionate feeling. But the humor and the appealing tenderness that delight us in *Petrushka* are gone.

Before continuing, a word should be said about the brief appearance of jazz in Mr. Stravinsky's second period. Mr. Mellers shrewdly explains how "the primitive element becomes a conscious sophistication of 20th-century jazz." But this would not for long suit an extremely sophisticated mind, and soon Mr. Stravinsky abandoned jazz, as indeed have all others, from Ravel to Copland, after an initial flirting. Since "sophisticated jazz" utilizes hand-me-down garments from the previous generation of "serious" composers, materials the Germans so expressively (and untranslatably) call *abgesunkenes Kulturgut,* any original creative artist will tire of it when he realizes the limitations it imposes on him. Such an artist can find nourishment in "cultural goods" that are eternally fresh, original, and "rising" — folk music — but not in those that are worn, derivative, and "sinking" — sophisticated jazz.

From here the road leads directly to the purely linear-contrapuntal, a trend that favored the "unemotional," "objective" game of dazzling virtuosity in manipulating voice-parts and instruments. The grotesque and the orgiastic, the tender and the lyrical — the *Symphony of Psalms* is a haunting pause in this trend — are now things of the past, yet neither the Russian period nor any of the subsequent Western periods represents a positive esthetic, a world view. It is impossible to consider the author of the *Autobiography,* or the *Poetics of Music,* or the co-author of the *Conversations* a musical esthete who formulates his theories in positive and concise doctrines. In the first place, in the latest of Robert Craft's inquests Mr. Stravinsky frankly admits that both his *Autobiography* and *Poetics* "were written through other people"; in the second place, the *obiter dicta* appearing in *Conversations* depend too much on Mr. Craft's coaching and editing. While many of the composer's pronouncements in the dialogues are distinguished by a robust common sense and immense knowledge of the *métier,* a certain looseness of thought, a harsh attitude towards fellow composers of all ages, as well as peremptory *ex cathedra* legislation on all matters and persons from antiquity to the present largely annul the pleasure caused by the treatment of the less controversial subjects. Mr. Stravinsky's appeals to history are not convincing either, and often bear little relation to actual events. He is sometimes in danger of being almost too learned a citizen of the world, of knowing too much musicology, too many literatures, sciences, and philosophies. The distinguished composer discusses these things with the utmost scientific seriousness, even using the lingo of modern psychology, physics, physiology, mathematics, and musicology; obviously he had the advantage of reviewing his ideas and materials in the light of recent contacts, directly through Mr. Craft, directly or indirectly through Messrs. Babbitt, Stockhausen, Boulez, and other matrimonial agencies that exist in order to bring fact and theory together. But time and again the unposed Stravinsky comes to the fore disclosing an attractive simplicity mercifully free of pretension, as when he speaks of his youth, of his early impressions — in a word, whenever he speaks of Russia as he knew her. What we see — when Mr. Craft permits it — is a longing for something that was really close to his heart, Russia and the heyday of his first sojourn in Paris, where the great ballets roused an enervated world unused to such vital and powerful music. What would have happened had Mr. Stravinsky stayed in Russia, in a Russia free from Marxist esthetics, or even had he become altogether a French composer? No one can tell, but the thought is fascinating. As we look at the Western Stravinsky, from the depth of his lonely soul there emerge poetic pictures, and yet he is not a poet, for in his marvelous and purely musical imagination manner usually triumphs over matter.

Of late he has turned to religious subjects — is he a genuinely religious composer of "sacred" music? No, he could not be, for his ideal world is too little concerned with the final inwardness of life. In reality, nowhere in the many works written since he became a representative of contemporary Western music was he able to transcend his egoism, therefore his spiritual center lies somewhere between dream and make-believe. A religiosity in which the last thing is missing cannot become altogether genuine. In the *Symphony of Psalms* Mr. Stravinsky surrendered himself with captivating awareness to the spirit of love he feels at the heart of life, a unique case in all his work. Mr. Mellers recognized this and expressed the distinction with penetrating insight when he said that in this work "the composer attains, in the last movement, to the love of God." Then he adds the reproach, gently but nonetheless positively, that in his later works Stravinsky "seems to be in love with the idea of God rather than with God himself." Perhaps this is also responsible for Mr. Stravinsky's amazing vacillation between styles and expressive means. Here he composes orgiastic revelry, there music based on severely objective intellectual notions and theories. But the theories are always revokable. Still, wherever he turns and whatever he composes he remains Stravinsky, the one and only lonesome, vain, and haughty Stravinsky. And one divines that in this highly personal ideal world of his he did not find real fulfillment, for everywhere there is missing a final truth; even in his dreams about himself. His "confessions" are the reflections of a monad, not the mirror of the world in the center of a creative soul. He does not live for others, and yet his art has become a program for a large part of the musical world.

THE USES OF CONVENTION: STRAVINSKY AND HIS MODELS

By EDWARD T. CONE

I

THE persisent vitality of conventional patterns in music has often been noted. Whatever the reasons for their original development, one advantage of their use is clear: in an art both abstract and temporal they furnish signposts to aid the listener, who can neither turn back nor pause to look around him. The danger, of course, is that the composer will use them as a crutch; and it is true that the academic conception of the forms as molds has encouraged the production of much facile and undistinguished music. But when, as during the period of the Viennese Classics, original musical thought and generally accepted procedures find not only mutual accommodation but mutual reinforcement, the results are happy for composer and audience alike.

The acceptance of conventions presents another possibility, which is my concern here. A composer may deliberately defeat the expectations aroused by the specific pattern followed; the resulting tension between the anticipated and the actual course of the music can be a source of esthetic delight. This is the way Stravinsky has used conventions — stylistic as well as narrowly "formal" — of the past, but it is important to realize that composers of the periods of interest to him have also played with their own conventions. A look at Haydn with this in mind will, I hope, not only increase our admiration for the earlier composer's musical intelligence and wit but also throw light on what Stravinsky has been doing.

First, however, a word about one element necessarily associated with any departure from accepted norms: surprise. Certainly Haydn intended the drumbeat in the "Surprise" Symphony to shock; and no doubt Beethoven was counting on more subtle reactions of the same kind when he began a symphony on an apparent dominant seventh and a concerto with a piano solo. But can any such effect escape being greatly diminished and even nullified by successive hearings? And is it possible for audiences today, after long familiarity, to experience to any degree the sensation of violated propriety apparently calculated by the composers?

Logically the answers should be "no." But just as, in seeing a suspense-filled play for the second time, we are so caught up in the flow of events that we allow ourselves to forget that we know what is coming next, so in following a skillfully written piece of music, however familiar, we can become so intent on what we are actually hearing that we do not anticipate exactly what is to come. When shocks occur under these circumstances, they are never so violent as before, but they register their artistic effect nevertheless. (To be sure, this solution does not apply to the Beethoven examples; but listeners trained to appreciate the historical effect of the cited openings can, paradoxically, even prepare themselves here to be caught off guard.)

The element of pure surprise is, after all, of minor esthetic interest. The considerations of real importance are that a deviation from the anticipated course should tell as a musically effective contrast, and that an apparently incongruous turn of events should prove to be integrally connected with the whole. These relations may become the clearer as the more visceral manifestations of shock subside. Their appreciation requires a high degree of musical sophistication on the part of the listener, and it is enlightening to contrast the kinds of knowledge presupposed by the cases about to be discussed. Haydn, writing for an eager audience that constantly demanded new works, could reasonably assume as his ideal hearer one familiar with every detail of the style of his own day; Stravinsky has to rely on the passive, historically oriented concertgoer of the 20th century.

II

Haydn's liberties with patterns he himself had so notably helped to establish are of two kinds. On the one hand, they may arise apparently spontaneously from the exigencies of the musical material, as when motivic development recasts the recapitulation of the first movement of Op. 76, No. 1. But in other cases the composer seems deliberately to play with the form—to use the pattern itself as a subject for creative development. Such treatment is a closer analogue to Stravinsky's, and for this reason I have chosen for analysis the finale of the Quartet Op. 54, No. 2.

It is probable that no printed program accompanied the performance of a new Haydn quartet, and in any event the listing of movements was not at that time a general practice. The Adagio of the finale, then, must have found an alert listener totally unprepared, since he would have been expecting the usual fast romp. How would he have taken the Adagio? No doubt as a typical slow introduction; and if so, he would have been guilty of the first of a series of mistaken interpretations, all encouraged by the composer and cleverly ordered in such a way that the subsequent correction of each merely exposes the listener to the next error. The introductory character of the opening motif is immediately thrown into question by the exact balance of the eight-measure period that it initiates; and when this entire section is repeated, one reinterprets it, not as an introduction but as the first statement of a song form. Wrong again! It *is* an introduction, although of an unusual kind, and the real song form begins with the first violin's new development of the opening motif over the slowly unfolding 'cello arpeggio that takes shape after measure 8-bis.

The three-part song form now develops so smoothly that suspicion is allayed — until the sudden turn to minor, emphasized by a succession of three barely disguised parallel fifths. The stand on the dominant that closes this section surely heralds a return to major, and obviously to another statement of the principal theme of the song form. The major appears, it is true; but nothing can be accepted as obvious in this movement. Now, when all hope of a fast finale has been given up, a Presto begins. Was the entire Adagio, huge as it was, an introduction after all? So the course of the Presto seems to suggest as it runs through its own three-part pattern in a manner typical of the openings of many Haydn rondos. But at the point where the first theme should normally come to a full cadence, to be followed by a contrast in key or mode (see, for example, the finale of Op. 50, No. 1) — just here the cadence is made deceptive, and it is followed by a dissolution with a pause on the dominant.

What can this mean? What follows is probably the single most original stroke in the entire movement. One might have foreseen a return to the theme of the slow song form, but surely not a reprise of the opening introductory period — a reprise at once so striking and so satisfying in effect as to bring home the realization that it was more than a mere introduction after all, since it is now bearing the weight of the recapitulation. And indeed when the expansive song of the first violin does return, it is in the nature of a coda, with its characteristic bow to the subdominant over a tonic pedal. Thus, although the design of the whole is established as a ternary Adagio with a Presto interlude, it is nevertheless unique. The apparently introductory period of the first statement assumes full thematic stature on its return; while the melody originally developed most fully is relegated to the coda.

It is useless to ask of this movement, "What 'form' is it in?" — useless but not irrelevant. Appreciation of the points discussed above requires that the listener be familiar with the conventions of the day; for the composer is constantly arousing expectations based thereon, and then defeating them — or fulfilling them in a novel way. He may even be poking fun at a pedantic insistence on regularity.

At the same time it is important to realize that he has created a new design, valid for these specific musical materials and comprehensible without reference to violated standards. From this point of view the movement can certainly be understood and enjoyed on its own terms. But the invited comparison between the unique pattern and the normal one leads to an awareness of the tension between them that sharpens one's perception of the extent to which Haydn has here widened the boundaries of his own style.

III

Stravinsky's preoccupation with the contrast between the idioms of earlier periods and those of his own is most obvious in works like *Pulcinella,* based on frankly borrowed materials; and one can certainly learn much about his methods from the way he adroitly and often comically reworks his sources. My concern, however, being the composer's use of stylistic and formal conventions, I have chosen a work based on a Classical model but without actual thematic quotation: the Symphony in C.

Unlike Haydn, Stravinsky could expect his audience to be more familiar with the musical language of the past than with that of the present — familiar enough, at any rate, to draw certain conclusions from the information furnished by programs he could normally (again unlike Haydn) expect them to be reading. What they would find there — the announcement of a symphony openly characterized as tonal, with four movements following the traditional order — would suggest a conservative, not to say reactionary, pastiche. (What they might have read previously in popular accounts of Stravinsky's "retrogression" would only confirm this surmise.) But these signposts would prove to be misleading guides for the unwary; and Stravinsky (this time like Haydn) may well have hoped that the more alert among his listeners might gain added enjoyment from the interplay of the anticipated and the actual.

Certainly the traditional framework is emphasized here: the Classical orchestral layout, the diatonic melodies, the metric regularity, the apparent harmonic simplicity, the ostensibly typical patterns. At the same time, any expectation of a work easily comprehensible in a comfortably familiar idiom is defeated, even for the most sanguine hearer, by certain immediately perceptible features: the distinctive instrumental sound; the persistent, though mild, dissonance; the sudden harmonic shifts; the peculiar heterophonic part-writing (most obvious in the second movement). Now, the simple filling-out of a Classical mold with contemporary stuffing could produce nothing more important than a parody in the manner of Prokofiev, but Stravinsky's intention is serious. He confronts the evoked historical manner at every point with his own version of contemporary language; the result is a complete reinterpretation and transformation of the earlier style.

A convincing demonstration of Stravinsky's method depends on closer analysis, for which I have chosen the opening *Moderato alla breve*. The traditional model here is clearly the sonata form; and as in the Fifth and Ninth Symphonies of Beethoven, an introduction adumbrates the first theme, which appears in proper form at m. 26. But the first measure, even as it (probably intentionally) recalls the opening of the Fifth, contradicts its ancestry by its reiteration, not of the dominant, but of the leading-tone; and the role of this leading-tone in the movement to come is one of the clearest indications of Stravinsky's intent. For the shock of this apparently incongruous detail is not produced for its own sake, or for the purpose of parody; it calls attention to the fundamental tonal ambiguity of the symphony: the tendency of B to act as a dominant rather than as a leading-tone. The consequent struggle between E and C is evident throughout the introduction, and the tonic established with the appearance of the theme in m. 26 retains the E as the bass of its first inversion. The E asserts its strength later at many crucial points: at the end of the exposition; at the false recapitulation, heralded by the establishment of the leading-tone of E; throughout the first half of the coda. Even the final chords of this movement and of the entire symphony retain the inverted form.

Another example of the new perspective on older procedures is the presentation of the first theme, recalling as it does the corresponding passage in Beethoven's First Symphony with its I-II-V sequence. With Beethoven the movement from each degree to the next is a clearly functional harmonic step; with Stravinsky these movements sound less like true progressions than like his characteristic harmonic shifts. There are several reasons for this effect. In the first place, the C-E ambiguity casts doubt even on the solidity of the tonic. This doubt extends to the dominant, which is also suspiciously tinged with the E coloring. Then there is the peculiar phrase-structure: extended, repetitive developments over an *ostinato* so nearly static that harmonic inflections within each phrase sound like incidents in the part-writing. Owing to the consequent absence of unambiguous harmonic cadences, clear phrase-divisions must be achieved by interruption and even by interpolation, as in mm. 39-42. As a result the function of the supertonic statement thus prepared is obscured, in contrast to the corresponding harmony in the Beethoven, unequivocally established by an applied dominant. When Stravinsky's dominant arrives (m. 48) it is heavily colored by the previously noted E. What we hear then, suggests the stepwise shift of I-II-III as an alternate and even more persuasive interpretation of an ostensibly functional I-II-V.

This typically Stravinskyan kind of harmonic motion explains much that happens later in the movement. Just as the I-II step of m. 43 is already hinted at in the inner voices of m. 30 and prophesied even more clearly in m. 35, so is it reflected on a large scale in mm. 61-93. This time the tendency of II to become a dominant is encouraged; but when the expected theme arrives, another stepwise shift takes place, silently as it were: IV replaces the long-prepared V. This substitution in turn permits another series of shifts (mm. 120-28), as a result of which V finally makes its appearance.

Perhaps the most interesting of Stravinsky's transformations is that of the sonata form itself. The Moderato adheres only superficially to the canons; its fundamental rhythm is of a different order. The clue is to be found in a striking crescendo that occurs twice. In the exposition, it is part of the bridge that heralds the second theme (mm. 74-93); in the recapitulation, now cut completely out of the accordingly reduced bridge, it recurs, suitably transposed, as a preparation for the coda (mm. 293-309). The passage is all the more noticeable for the sudden pause that follows it each time, and its displacement cannot go unremarked. This parallelism between two passages that, in the usual sonata movement, would not correspond, points to a unique structure. Accepting the pauses as important points of articulation, I suggest the following divisions, more natural for this movement than the standard ones, and startling in the close parallel of their proportions:

Begins on m. 1   26   60   74   ‖   94
            Intro.   Th. I   Bridge A — B   Th. II
                      ⎵_____⎵
                              93 mm.   58 mm.

            m. 152
            Development
            67½ mm.

m. 219   225   261   276   293 ‖ 310   344
Trans.   Th. I   Bridge A   Th. II   Bridge B ‖ Coda X — Y
       ⎵_____⎵
                    90½ mm.   59 mm.

(Notes on the above:

1. I have included the transition of mm. 219-25 in the recapitulation, because it furnished an upbeat to Theme I corresponding to the introduction.

2. I have included a few measures of upbeat each time as the beginning of Theme II.

3. In spite of the empty measure at m. 148, I have regarded the next three measures as constituting the cadence of the exposition. There is a close parallel here to the end of the movement.)

The balance of the movement, then, is not of exposition against recapitulation, but rather of the exposition on the one side against the recapitulation plus coda on the other. Not only does the second theme in the exposition balance the coda, but the internal divisions of the two sections show close parallels. The second theme, beginning in IV, moves to V at m. 128, the resulting division being 34-24 measures (of which the last three are cadential chords). The coda is divided by the reappearance of Theme I in the proportions 34-25 measures (of which the last five are cadential chords).

The subdivision of Theme II in the exposition brings to light another structure, one even more at odds with the progressive development inherent in the Classical form. Embedded within the more obvious parallel balance is a completely symmetrical layout:

Intro.	Th. I	Bridge	Theme II C	—	D
25 mm.	34 mm.	34 mm.	34 mm.		24 mm.

This fails of being a perfect arch by only one measure. Nor is this all. The shortened and altered recapitulation is susceptible of less subdivision than the more relaxed exposition, and I think that the score here can be shown to justify the cluster of Transition-Theme I-Bridge A as one group and Theme II-Bridge B as another. If these are accepted, the entire movement takes on the shape of a huge arch. Such a symmetrical ordering paradoxically appears to contradict the previously outlined balance of parallel sections; yet the composer undoubtedly meant this alternative plan to be heard. The correspondence of the beginning and the end is apparent, for both Theme I in the exposition and Coda X are divided by pauses into twice 17 measures. An analogous pause in the recapitulation at m. 243, now the most obvious articulation in Group I, produces a division matching that of Theme II in the exposition. These subdivisions, indicated by parentheses, underline the symmetry of the following plan, in which each leg of the central arch is itself a smaller arch:

Intro.	Th. I	Br.	Th. II	Dev.	Group I	Group II	Coda X	—	Y
25 mm.	34 mm.	34 mm.	58 mm.	67½ mm.	56½ mm.	34 mm.	34 mm.		25 mm.
	(2x17)		(34 + 24)		(24½ + 32)		(2 x 17)		

The development is, of course, virtually twice 34 measures. This is the middle of the movement, and perched square on the center (mm. 181-90) is the false recapitulation! The proportions of the movement are thus roughly:

$$5 — 7 — 7 — 12 \quad — \quad 14 \quad — \quad 12 \quad — 7 — 7 — 5$$
$$(7 + 5) \quad (2 \times 7) \quad (5 + 7)$$

A close examination of the phrase-structure will disclose, even in the details, a remarkably consistent adherence to ratios derived from these numbers.

What is the importance of all this? It is twofold. First, a scheme of this kind affords a clue to the problem of Stravinsky's harmonic rhythm, since it offers a rationale for his choice of turning-points between harmonic areas. Further, it indicates a reason for Stravinsky's interest in the 18th-century framework. The Classical balance of phrases and periods, so carefully adjusted to the demands of functional tonality, becomes an analogue for the organization of his own kind of diatonicism. But the typical Classical balance, even when apparently rigid, controlled contrasting events moving at varying speeds, so that the listener's experience usually belied the exact parallel of the time-spans and defeated most attempts to measure one against the other. Stravinsky's sections — rhythmically persistent, harmonically static, melodically circular — not only invite the hearer to make the comparisons leading to just such measurement, but also reward him for doing so. Far from exploiting the sonata form as the traditional vehicle for realizing the musical or dramatic potentialities of tonal conflict and progression, he adapts it to his own perennial purpose: the articulated division of a uniform temporal flow.

IV

Haydn was attacking certain conventional presuppositions of the Classical style from the inside, since he had grown up within it — or rather, it had grown around him. Almost every moment in his quartet movement represents a questioning, a reexamination of these standards, and in every case the solution avoids the obvious on the one side and the arbitrary on the other. It is a narrow path, but one that Haydn maintains successfully to his goal: a broader redefinition of his own style.

Stravinsky, approaching the Classical from outside, as a historically defined manner, superficially follows its conventions more closely than Haydn. The influence of his personal idiom, however, is so strong that the resulting reinterpretation goes far beyond that of the earlier composer. The result is not an extension but a transformation of his model.

Now, it is interesting to see the same kind of force at work when Stravinsky turns to an idiom of his own day. When he uses the twelve-tone method it is again, so to speak, as an outsider adopting a historically defined mode. Since what he is now appropriating is not a generalized plan of formal organization but a detailed technique that necessarily influences the choice of every note, the analogy must not be pushed too far; still, it will be instructive to contrast briefly Stravinsky's handling of a few aspects of the new conventions with that of one who had eminently developed them.

By the time Schoenberg came to write his late works, he was manipulating his tone-rows in a way that, while very free, nevertheless always respected the basic structural role of the series. In the String Trio, for example, the ordering of the notes varies greatly in detail, but the fundamental hexachords are rarely violated. Again, Schoenberg feels under no compunction to state the entire row in canonical form at the outset, so long as its basic properties are clear. In the Phantasy, Opus 47, the appearance of the second hexachord is delayed until m. 10, and only in mm. 32-33 is the row given its first unequivocal statement. But these apparent licenses reveal the interaction between the general method and the specific formal demands. The second hexachord punctuates an important phrase-division, and the entire row underlines the brief reprise that closes off the first section. Throughout these works, the important divisions of phrases, periods, and sections are emphasized in just such ways; and both the twelve-tone texture and the rhythmic shape gain clarity by this mutual reinforcement.

In the case of Stravinsky's *Movements* for Piano and Orchestra, it is obvious from the start that his use of the system is divergent. After an initial statement, the row is promptly obscured — obscured in such a way by orchestral doublings, note-repetitions, and changes of order that its profile becomes unclear and its structural function doubtful. Doubtful it should be, for in m. 7 there emerges a series (not of twelve tones, for there are many repetitions), motivically related to but derived in no conventional way from the original, and vying with it in importance. The new series is completely stated three times during the first half of this movement, only to disappear into the tone-row from which it came. At this point it is already evident that Stravinsky's concern with the twelve-tone system is more with its vocabulary and texture than with its structure. Earlier, the Classical framework was an aid in the control of a preponderantly diatonic language; now the new mode offers an even closer control of chromaticism, and serves as a source of material as well.

The real structure, now as before, remains his own. What that is can be seen most clearly through his use of well-defined instrumental colors to mark important divisions: the trumpet that precedes and follows the piano's initial statement; the contrast of the three statements of the subsidiary series — piano virtually alone, flute, and piano with plucked strings; the sustained 'cello harmonic that closes the section; the trombones that begin the second half. Stravinsky is proceeding here, as before, with clearly marked portions of time, but his former harmonically static blocks of sound have given way to a more pliant, elastic, chromatic polyphony. Look for example at the three strokes of the harp that accentuate the pauses in the piano line of m. 42. These form a kind of instrumental *ostinato* by the introduction of a static, unifying tone-color; at the same time they are moving in pitch— in fact, they are inaugurating a new statement of the series. Again, the transitional passages connecting each movement with the next are sometimes clearly explicable as twelve-tone units, sometimes not; but they are always easily perceptible instrumental units, set off from the main body of the work as contrasting blocks, and each orchestrally differentiated from the others.

Occasionally Stravinsky reverts even now to a true pedal or *ostinato* (although less frequently than in *Canticum sacrum* and *Threni*). Here again a comparison with Schoenberg may be of value. The passage beginning with m. 40 of the Phantasy shows how an *ostinato* accompaniment figure can be logically introduced within a twelve-tone context. The melody in the violin runs through one hexachord; the *ostinato* in the piano is based entirely on its complementary inversion. The *ostinato* is composed of two two-note motifs, to which a third motif is soon added; in terms of the row, they are made up of elements 1-2, 3-4, and 5-6 respectively. Thus within each hexachord the ordering is preserved; and because the hexachords are mutually complementary, no casual doublings can occur in spite of the continued *ostinato*. When the melody moves on to another hexachord, the accompaniment shifts correspondingly.

Contrast this technique, developed from the exigencies of the system itself, with that of Stravinsky in *Movements* IV, which throws the piano part into relief against a series of static four-note chords in string harmonics. Each of these chords is derived in the same way: by the sustaining of elements 3-4 and 7-8 of a stated row (retrograde-inversion the first and third times, inversion the second). Thus the ordering is not preserved, for these four notes are not normally adjacent. Furthermore, since complete statements are sounded against each chord, fortuitous doublings are inescapable. Unlike the Schoenberg *ostinato,* which defines a thematic phrase by completing the twelve-tone aggregate, these act as harmonic poles to support a symmetrical division into three time-blocks. It is ironic that this movement, the clearest of all in its derivation from the tone-row, should depart so far in its over-all structure from usually accepted twelve-tone ideals.

V

The contrast between Schoenberg and Stravinsky is roughly analogous to the one involving Haydn. Schoenberg, like Haydn, modified the conventions and extended the techniques of his musical language from within — from the vantage ground of one who had played a preeminent role in the shaping of the language in the first place. Stravinsky, approaching each from without, reinterprets and transforms it so radically to fit his own needs that it remains only superficially related to the original.

If this were all, Stravinsky would have become at most an interesting mannerist, and an inconstant one at that. But this is not all. What has been omitted — or only hinted at up to now — is of crucial importance: the relation of manner and mannerism to style. Style is the vitality that comes from the integrated and balanced interaction of all the dimensions of an art. By manner I mean a style, whether of the past or of the present, viewed reductively as rigidly defined and historically restricted. Mannerism is the result of the personal appropriation of such a manner, with the frequent concomitants of exaggeration, distortion, and fragmentation. What Stravinsky has demonstrated convincingly is the feasibility of putting manneristic elements to good use in the service of a powerful style.

This discussion has been misleading insofar as it has implied that Stravinsky's borrowings from past and present and their distortion at his hands are the chief sources of interest in his music. I now suggest that exactly the reverse is true: that the fate of these adopted elements, although a matter of legitimate esthetic concern, is nevertheless secondary to their real value: their influence on his own highly individual musical image. With Stravinsky, as with Haydn and Schoenberg, the contrast between the expectations aroused by the accepted conventions and the actual use to which they are put produces tension — but with Stravinsky, the resultant pull is in a different direction. In listening to the Haydn and Schoenberg examples we are engrossed by the way in which the personal style is constantly reshaping the general convention. We should hear Stravinsky in just the opposite sense: what is of prime importance is how the borrowed convention extends and modifies the personal style.

We have already come to hear the neo-Classical works in this way, and that is why the Symphony in C and other compositions of its period are now, after years of attack as parodistic pastiches, being recognized as masterpieces. No doubt one day we shall be able to hear the recent works in the same way. Stravinsky's style is too strong and too individual to permit long disguise. To watch it preserve its identity through all its adventures is endlessly fascinating.

STRAVINSKY'S OEDIPUS
AS 20TH-CENTURY HERO

By WILFRID MELLERS

IF we accept Stravinsky as the most "central" representative of 20th-century music, we have to admit that he is representative in a paradoxical way. For just as he has expressed himself through a deliberate denial of what we are accustomed to call expression, so he has been representative by turning his back on most of the values and assumptions that have gone to make us what we are. This suggests that we too are at least subconsciously distrustful of the beliefs in which we have been nurtured. The Stravinskian dubiety is also ours: which matters because his art's admission of dubiety is more honest, less afraid, than most of us can hope to be.

We live at the end of a civilization that, starting with the European Renaissance, has been based on man's belief in his ability to control his own destiny; this ability he has attained, or thinks he has attained, through reason and through the power over the natural world that reason gives him. The "natural world" includes, of course, man's own nature; and the preoccupation of post-Renaissance art with expression and communication has been largely a manifestation of the belief that man, through the ordering of his own passions, may influence the emotions, and ultimately the behavior, of other people: so that the artist's personal expression is also a social force. Now Stravinsky — partly because Russia bypassed the European Renaissance — has never accepted music as expression and communication in this sense. For him, music has always been ritual, even though, as a modern man twice deracinated, he has lived in societies that have forgotten what ritual means. In early works like *The Rite of Spring* and *The Wedding* he was able, being a Russian, to re-invoke the ritual of a remote and primitive past. In so doing he was performing a negative and a positive act simultaneously: negative because the terror and the violence in the ritual seemed directly to parallel the death-struggle of our deracinated civilization which was then erupting in the first of the World Wars; positive because this primitive vitality served as a reminder of the instinctive passional life that modern man had lost. From this point of view we had to recognize, of course, that the ritual wasn't true. We could not live it, we could only act it: which is why the ritual was to be objectified in the conscious artifice of ballet. Classical (Tchaikovskian) ballet had been essentially an artifice of dream in which the perturbations of real life could be momently resolved. Stravinsky's *Wedding* is a dream too, though the human reality it starts from is, deliberately, more rudimentary. "Let's pretend," it says, that we self-conscious beings of the 20th century can enter into man's instinctive animal nature and can — at the end — experience his spontaneous yearning for the unity that is love. But the "geometric" pattern-making of the music, the abstract black and white choreography, admits that the artifice is a pretence. The game, though a game, is still beautiful, its effect cathartic.

The burden of consciousness cannot, however, be brushed aside merely by a revocation of the primitive springs of life; and that Stravinsky was aware of this is suggested by the fact that, in war-time works such as *The Soldier's Tale,* the theme of human guilt and responsibility makes a somewhat queasy appearance in a puppet-like parody of the Faust legend. Techniques and conventions from widely separated bits of Europe's "humanist" past are disturbingly re-integrated, while the primitive element becomes a conscious sophistication of 20th-century jazz. The queasiness, even the cynicism, were serious enough in purpose and effect; and had positive direction in that they led Stravinsky to explore — in the "neo-Classic" works of his middle years — his relationship to the great humanist tradition. Like his Renaissance and Baroque predecessors, he took his themes from classical antiquity, rather than from Christian tradition, for he did not wish, at this point, to be concerned with a dichotomy between spirit and flesh. He started from those conventions whereby men of the Baroque world had conveyed their belief that Man might be Hero, even to the point of divinity. In effect, however, he inverted the significance that these conventions had had at the time when they were created. This process we can examine in Stravinsky's opera *Oedipus Rex,* perhaps the key work in his long career, and the only one to make *direct* use of the conventions of Baroque opera, wherein the humanist attempted man's deification.

A real heroic opera — and this applies too to Handel's oratorios, which are heroic operas on biblical subjects — was simultaneously a ritual of humanism (a masque or State ceremonial) and a drama dealing with the perversity of man's passions, which makes paradise-on-earth a difficult ideal. Stravinsky preserves the "heroic" closed aria form and also the atmosphere of ritual ceremony. At the same time he admits that we can hardly belong to this ritual, any more than we

could share in the primitive ritual of *The Wedding*; and this he symbo-
lizes by returning to the (authentically Greek) stylization of the mask,
and by having the opera acted and sung in a dead language (Latin),
interspersed with narration in modern French, by a man in modern
evening dress (in the original performances by Cocteau himself, the
librettist). This smart, nineteen-twentyish convention becomes, in the
hands of a master at the height of his powers, unexpectedly moving.
It tells us that we, like the narrator, are cut off from the springs of
passion and from the humanist's celebration; then gradually, as the
tragedy unfolds, we come to realize that it is our tragedy after all. We
may not be kings, great or noble as is Oedipus, but we too are subject
to the destiny that hounds us; and it is only our pride that prevents us
from seeing that destiny is the guilt within us all. From this point of
view it is significant that Stravinsky chose, for this central work in his
career, a myth that the more buoyant humanists of the heroic age had
preferred to leave alone. His Oedipus deals directly with the ego's
pride: but also with the ego's insufficiency. This is why the humanist
ritual of the opera is linked both with the primitive ritual of earlier
works and with the religious ritual of his later, quasi-liturgical pieces.

After the spoken Prologue, in which Cocteau recounts the story
in modern French, the chorus, masked like living statues, sing of the
plague that ravages Thebes. They are the men of the city, but also
Mankind, whose burden of suffering is a burden of guilt. The anti-
expressive syllabic recitation, the *ostinato* patterns over chugging B-flat
minor thirds, have affinities with Stravinsky's primitive phase, yet the
effect is not one of orgiastic excitement. Indeed, falling minor thirds
have always been a musical synonym for the domination of earth and
therefore of death (consider the late works of Brahms); and the feeling
here is of almost claustrophobic constriction, of a submission to fate
that may be equated with submission to death. Although we are not
as yet aware of the significance of the twofold relationship, we sense,
as we listen, that this music is complementary both to the primitive
pieces and also to the Christian liturgical works that, at this time,
Stravinsky was composing for the Russian Orthodox Church.

In this grand, static lamentation there is virtually no harmonic movement, though there is much harmonic tension, mainly created by the
telescoping of tonic, dominant, and subdominant chords. There is a hint
of very slow momentum as the chorus — in increasingly disjointed rhythm
over nagging thirds — call on their King, Oedipus, to help them; until

out of the prison of the falling thirds a prancing, dotted-rhythmed phrase is generated, and Oedipus, a high heroic tenor, sings in ornate coloratura "Ego Oedipus" — I, Oedipus, will free you. Although the coloratura suggests the sublime assurance of the god-king, and derives from the ornamentation of Baroque opera, there is also a quality — in the high register and the oscillations around a fixed point — that reminds us of liturgical incantation:

Ex. 1

And Oedipus's freedom seems to be itself imprisoned, not only by the nodal oscillations of his vocal line, but also by a slowly revolving *ostinato* in the bass that chains down the clarinets' prancing arpeggios and reasserts the B-flat minor obsession, against the voice's aspiration to C. Indeed, the fateful minor thirds continue intermittently, and are fully re-established in the *Serva* chorus, in which the men of Thebes ask their leader what is to be done that they may be delivered.

Oedipus says that Creon, the Queen's brother, has just returned from Delphi, where he has been to consult the oracles. Immediately the B-flat minor obsession is banished. Sonorous G major chords from the chorus welcome Creon in hopeful luminosity; as they become ordinary men, looking towards their potential everyday activities, their music loses its monumentally tragic quality and becomes somewhat primitively Mussorgskian, for they, like us, are not kings. Creon, being at this stage a representative of the gods, sings a strict *da capo* aria: in which there can be no development since perfection is unalterable. But there's a certain ambivalence in his music, as there was in the heroic aria of the Baroque age itself. The middle section of the aria, touching on F minor, hints at the B-flat minor obsession as it refers to the old, dead king, while there is something frenzied about the C major assertiveness of the aria itself. The widely arpeggiated tune is crude, even cruel, with the brass-band vigor of early Verdi rather than the grandeur of Handel; and the rhythmic *ostinato* on four horns suggests a pre-conscious terror beneath the surface. The man-god complacence carries all before it, however. After he has informed the chorus that the oracles report that the murderer of their former king Laius is among them and must be discovered, Creon concludes with a tremendous C major arpeggio: *Apollo dixit deus.*

Oedipus, as leader, responds to the challenge. He boasts of his skill in solving riddles, which stands as a symbol of man's ability to control his destiny through reason; and promises to save his people by discovering the murderer. This aria, which is in E-flat (the opera's man-key, as opposed to C major, which is the key of the gods), is an almost hysterical intensification of his earlier ornate style. Beginning with prideful arpeggiated phrases which emulate those of Creon, it turns into more emotionally agitated sevenths, emphasizing in tipsy narcissism the word "ego" as it sweeps into oscillating coloratura:

Ex. 2

Over the sustained E-flat bass the voice resolves the fourth on to the prideful major third; but although the music is superb in the strict sense,

the chorus seem to suspect that there is something a little phoney about
it. Their reiterated "deus dixit tibi" phrase is metamorphosed back into
the fateful minor thirds, now screwed up a semitone into B minor;
and after invoking the gods Minerva, Diana, Phoebus, and Bacchus,
they call on Tiresias, blind prophet who sees in the dark, since he
would be more likely to help them than a human leader, however mighty.
In liturgically solemn repeated notes and widespread arpeggio figurations, oscillating tonally between Man's E-flat and God's C major,
Tiresias says that he will not, cannot, reveal the truth. Oedipus, his im-
perturbability threatened, taunts Tiresias: whereupon, in a line of immense, superhuman range, Tiresias announces that the King's murderer
is a King. For the first time the tonality hints — by way of a C major-
A minor ambiguity that merges into G — at D major, with a resonant
triad on horns reinforced by double basses in octaves.

At the moment we don't realize the significance of this: for Oedipus
takes over the sustained D-natural, only to force it back to his man-key
of E-flat. Yet though Oedipus has been ruffled by his encounter with
Tiresias, it marks a stage in his spiritual pilgrimage, and his second
E-flat aria is only superficially similar to the first. Though the line is
derived from his "superb" aria, it is now broken, chromatic, even
fragmentary. For the first time he reveals his weakness, which is also
his humanity, accusing Creon and Tiresias of plotting against him,
bragging of his abilities as riddle-solver, appealing to the chorus not to
forget his previous triumphs; so his proud line now carries harmonic
implications that imbue it with pathos, even tenderness:

Ex. 3

I - nvi - di - a for - tu - nam o - dit,

cre - a - vi - stis me re - gem.

Significantly, he ends unaccompanied, singing the *chorus's* falling minor
thirds, and in C minor, relative of E-flat and halfway to the god-key
which is C major.

Ex. 4

Vo-lunt re-gem pe-ri-re,ves-trum re-gem pe-ri-re,cla-rum Œ-di-po-dem,ves-trum re-gem.

In seeing himself as one with the many he proceeds from pride to humility; begins, tremulously, hesitantly, to accept fate and death in his music, if not in his words. It is interesting that formally this song is not a *da capo* aria but a rondo in which the episodes change the destiny of the theme. His absolutism disintegrates, even while he tries to assert it. This is why the act can conclude with a Gloria, celebrating Jocasta's arrival in Stravinsky's "white note" diatonicism. The personal life of Oedipus's rondo-aria is banished; but the ceremonial music that succeeds is related more to Stravinsky's music for the Russian Orthodox Church and even to his primitive works than to the harmonic ceremonial of a heroic composer such as Handel. Indeed, the chorus strikingly anticipates the *Symphony of Psalms*.

Oedipus's rondo-aria, which has more harmonic movement than any previous music in the opera, and the consequent Gloria, which has no harmonic movement at all, make together the axis on which the work revolves. The Gloria concludes the first Act, and is repeated as prelude to the second: which follows the path to self-knowledge. To begin with, Jocasta pours scorn on all oracles. Her music hasn't the rigid, frigid panache that comes of Oedipus's desire for self-deification; it has a human, almost Verdian, lyrical sweep and a harmonic momentum such as Oedipus acquires only in his rondo. The key, G minor, is dominant of the godly C, relative of the fateful B-flat; her reiterated syncopations and chromatic intensifications suggest an essentially human defiance. Defiance, in the F major middle section of the *da capo* form,

Ex. 5

turns into insolent ridicule. To chattering clarinet triplets she points out how oracles often lie, and must do in this case, for the old king was killed twelve years ago, outside the town, by the crossroads. The repeated eighth-note figuration sounds panic-stricken, however; and when the *da capo* returns the syncopations and chromatics affect us differently, seeming to be dragging and anguished rather than defiant. At this point we realize that the minor thirds pad unobtrusively beneath the impassioned lyricism. She too struggles against destiny; and if, being a woman, she is more immediately human than Oedipus she is also less heroic, and is not, like him, absolved.

Oedipus's assurance is finally shaken by Jocasta's reference to the past, for he recalls that twelve years ago he killed a stranger at the crossroads. Hypnotically, the chorus takes up the word "trivium," hammering it into Oedipus's mind. *Ego senem kekidi*, he stammers, to a phrase that inverts the falling thirds, accompanied only by terrifying C minor thirds on the timpani:

Ex. 6

This is the moment of self-revelation, when he sees that the guilt is within; and at first the revelation leads to chaos, only just held in check by the rigidity of the *ostinato* pattern. Jocasta screams in wild 12/8 chromatics that the oracles always lie: while Oedipus sings in duo a strange, bewildered, broken lament, confessing his past history. So the mother-wife and the son-husband sing together, in C minor, relative of the man-key E-flat, tonic minor of the god-key C major: on which a B-flat *ostinato* closes remorselessly, as Oedipus says that, though afraid, he must know the truth, must see the shepherd who was the only witness of his crime.

An anonymous messenger, agent of destiny, enters to reveal that Oedipus's reputed father, Polybus, has died, admitting that Oedipus was an adopted son. The messenger, being a low, unheroic character, sings a Mussorgskian peasant-like incantation, oscillating around a nodal point. The chorus take up the words *falsus pater,* stuttering, horror-struck; words, line, and rhythm are all broken, the harmonic movement gelid:

Ex. 7

Momentarily, when the messenger tells them that Oedipus was found as a baby on Mount Citheron, with his feet pierced, the chorus sing in modal innocence that a miracle is about to be revealed: he will prove to be born of a goddess. But the shepherd-witness comes forward to reveal the truth. In a swaying arioso that, like Oedipus's "kekidi" phrase, inverts the falling thirds, he carries the music back to the obsessive B-flat minor. The shepherd's aria, accompanied only by two bassoons and then·timpani, induces a state of trance in everyone except Jocasta who, now knowing that she is the wife of her own son, who was his father's murderer, rushes out.

Oedipus thinks, or pretends to think, that Jocasta has gone off in shame at the discovery of his lowly birth. He makes a desperate return to his early arrogance and sings a scornful Italianate aria over a bouncing bass. The key, F major, is the same as the insolent middle section of Jocasta's first aria, and perhaps it is not an accident that F is the dominant of fate's B-flat. But the human impulse to dominate is now frantic indeed, as is suggested by the jaunty vivacity of the dotted rhythm that takes us back to Oedipus's first appearance. The coloratura has here a kind of horrifying inanity, as though Oedipus is trying to cheer himself up, against all odds. The aria concludes in a cadenza of hysterical exultation, in wild descending chromatics that carry us, however, from F major to D minor. At this point the thudding minor thirds return, along with the hammering *kekidi* rhythm; and we realize that his exultation, though a mask, has not been entirely synthetic. Messenger, shepherd, and chorus declaim the truth on repeated D's; woodwind and strings alternate to the *kekidi* rhythm in false relations between D major and minor; and Oedipus chants a brief arioso which, beginning in B minor over the pedal D's, miraculously transforms the falling minor thirds into D major on the words *lux facta est:*

Ex. 8

Light floods his spirit as he decides to put out the light of his eyes; and like Shakespeare's Gloucester in *King Lear* he could' say "I stumbled when I saw." So Stravinsky stresses the Christian implications that he can discover in the myth; and it is relevant to note that Oedipus's final arioso is closer to liturgical chant than it is to the heroic music he has sung previously. Or rather one could say that at the end he rediscovers the music that was implicit in his first utterance, which is now purged of egoism and self-will.

The transformation of the falling thirds into D major is the fulfillment of Tiresias's prophecy, which had also ended with a D major triad. Then the triad had been immediately contradicted by Oedipus's E-flat egoism; now it is Oedipus himself who initiates the miraculous metamorphosis. The opera is dominated by the search for D major, which is the key of the inner light; and the tonal scheme of the work has a symmetry that is simultaneously musical and doctrinal. One can notate this in a kind of cyclical chart:

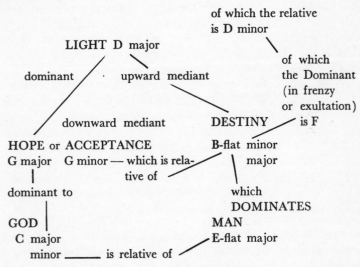

Stravinsky adheres to this scheme with consistency; and that he almost certainly did so without conscious intent emphasizes how instinctively he thinks and feels in ritualistic and "doctrinal" terms. The discovery of Light is the consummation of the tragedy; but an epilogue is needed to place the revelation in the context of our lives. So the visionary moment is followed immediately by a trumpet fanfare in a tonally ambiguous region between B-flat major and G minor (see chart). The Messenger announces that Jocasta has hanged herself, and the chorus takes up his words, proceeding to tell us, in a sickening, lurching six-eight rhythm, how Oedipus has blinded himself with a golden pin from her dress. The key is a compromise between C minor and E-flat major, for it is his and our humanity, not the moment of revelation, that we are now concerned with. The bass tends to oscillate around the E-flat pedal; but the vocal lines are tense with upward-thrusting chromatics and major-minor ambiguities. Significantly, the music refers back to the C minor duo of horror and bewilderment that Oedipus and Jocasta had sung at the moment of discovery, for we know that we are involved in their doom.

After each phase of the narration of the suicide and self-blinding, the trumpet fanfares return, in rondo style: so that the human tragedy is given an epic impersonality. After each fanfare the instrumental texture that accompanies the chorus becomes more agitated, ending with scalewise whirling sixteenth notes. On the words "spectaculum omnium atrocissimum" the C minor-E-flat major ambiguity seems to resolve itself into a solemn brass cadence on the D major triad. This acts, however, as a dominant to G minor: in which key the upward shooting scales of the opera's opening are reinstated. (These scales are derived from the French overture of the heroic age, though they have become terrifying rather than pompously magisterial.) Oedipus totters in, blind, and the chorus says farewell to him, who carries their guilt as well as his own. Gradually the thudding minor thirds of the fate-motif take over, now pulled down by the weight of sorrow from B-flat minor to G minor — dominant of the god-key C, as B-flat is dominant of the man-key E-flat. As the minor thirds fade out on 'cellos, double basses, and timpani, the opera tells us that, though man is "dominated" by destiny, he may find his divine redemption. G minor is the relative of B-flat: but also the gateway to light, which is D.

The Christian, rather than humanistic, implications of Stravinsky's heroic opera are fulfilled in the sequence of works that follows, and most notably in the *Symphony of Psalms,* which has claims to be considered his masterwork. In this work he again starts from the Baroque conventions of toccata and fugue. The similarity to Baroque techniques is, however, no more than superficial: for the work shows little evidence of the Baroque sense of harmonic momentum. Indeed, in so far as the themes tend to oscillate around a nodal point and the structures to be organized by linear and rhythmic pattern rather than by harmonic and tonal architecture, the Symphony is strictly comparable with some aspects of medieval technique; and the seemingly pre-ordained or "doctrinal" system of key-relationships is also in principle, if not in practice, appropriate to an age of faith. And here, in the marvelous lyrical expansion of the last movement, the faith is fulfilled, the music being at once an evocation of "the chime and symphony of Nature" and an act of worship.

So the third phase of Stravinsky's career was already implicit in the *Symphony of Psalms,* which was, in turn, inherent in *Oedipus Rex.* This third phase begins with works such as the Mass and the Cantata wherein, starting from medieval texts, he consciously borrows medieval techniques also — the non-harmonic, nodal *ostinato,* the pre-ordained, "doctrinal" serialism. His final acceptance of Webern's complete chromatic serialization is a logical extension of this neo-medieval serialism; and it has been frequently pointed out that Stravinsky does not employ his rows in a Webernesque spirit but in a more literal sense — in much the same way as a medieval composer used his *cantus firmus* as the Word. The difference, of course, lies in the fact that the *cantus firmus* did have doctrinal significance which was intelligible to at least a fair proportion of the people who listened to, participated in, the music. Stravinsky's Word is a private invention; and since we do not live in an age of faith we cannot participate in a ritual, or at least not on the terms in which it is offered to us. One may question, too, whether Stravinsky's music has ever again achieved the lyrical fulfillment it reaches in the *Symphony of Psalms.* That work, which is certainly among the two or three supreme masterpieces of the 20th century, is a revelation of God's love because the creator attains, in the last movement, to the love of God. In comparison, Stravinsky's later works seem to be in love with the idea of God, rather than with God Himself; and in this too he may well be "representative." There hasn't been a great religious composer since (in their different but complementary ways) late Beethoven and Bruckner; and one would hardly expect such a composer, in the world we have made. None the less, the great, central composers of our time have been seekers. Schoenberg, starting from an awareness of chaos and disintegration both within the psyche and in the external world, thought of himself as a Moses who tried, but failed, to lead his people into the Promised Land; Stravinsky, in *Oedipus Rex* and the *Symphony of Psalms,* admitted to the humanist's burden of guilt and had his momentary vision of redemption. In both cases, the creator started from man-as-he-is. Deliberately to reject our humanistic birthright, however, carries graver and more dangerous implications: for it is easy to mistake the rite itself for the vision that it should make incarnate. This may be true of some — by no means all — of Stravinsky's later works, and is certainly true of a fair proportion of post-Webern serialism, though never of Webern himself, who was, and intended to be, both a mystical and a post-Renaissance "expressive" composer.

If a criticism seems to be implied in the previous paragraph, it is not a criticism of Stravinsky. There is a deeply allegorical significance in the fact that he, our spokesman, should be in a sense a composer of denial; and we know that although the rite has not always been, with him, an act of incarnation, it has been a historical necessity: the consequence of an agonizing awareness of the "human predicament." He has come to accept as historical necessity the fragmentation of line and the disintegration of rhythm; and he must know that something very similar has occurred before in European history — at the expiring twilight of the Middle Ages — and that these late medieval linear and rhythmic contortions now seem grotesque rather than life-enhancing. They were not the creative essence of the Middle Ages which—supremely in Gregorian chant — has expressed the fundamental human instinct for flow and continuity, following the heartbeat, but aspiring to an airborne ecstacy. Yet the later dislocations were a "necessity," as was the imposition of an ever more rigid external authority, if we were to be rescued from chaos. Doubtless the 20th-century dislocations are necessary too; and we certainly cannot doubt the probity of Stravinsky's "authority" even though, being man-made rather than god-given, its purpose and destiny are obscure. And we listen with the deeper respect because we remember that — especially in the work of his middle years — Stravinsky has shown us that, even in our bruised and battered world, the heart may still sing in the sustained lyrical period, the pulse beat in a rhythm that is not motorized, but fluid and compulsive as the sea. When it happens, it's both true and miraculous: for Stravinsky's "representative" significance lies in the fact that he is not by nature a lyrical composer.

STRAVINSKY AND TCHAIKOVSKY:
LE BAISER DE LA FÉE

By LAWRENCE MORTON

STRAVINSKY'S admiration of Tchaikovsky began in childhood. It could have been initiated by the St. Petersburg productions of the latter's ballets, *The Sleeping Beauty* having been performed there in January 1890, *The Nutcracker* in December 1892. The Stravinsky household boasted a photograph of the composer inscribed to Igor's father as a memento of his performance of the role of the monk in *The Sorceress*. Household conversation too must have encouraged the boy's reverence for so great a master as Tchaikovsky was held to be. One of young Igor's unforgettable experiences was seeing the great man in person at the Maryinsky Theater at the fiftieth-anniversary performance of *Russlan and Ludmilla* — two weeks later Tchaikovsky was dead. Later, while studying with Rimsky-Korsakov (who must necessarily have been critical of his rival for first place among Russian composers), Stravinsky continued to nourish his love for Tchaikovsky's music. Through the years, this admiration remained an article of musical faith, though surely its intensity must have varied. Its high point was reached during the 1920s, beginning with Diaghilev's great production of *The Sleeping Beauty* in London. Stravinsky participated in this revival. He orchestrated a few numbers which, having been cut at the Tsar's suggestion after the first performance, were consequently omitted from the published edition. Perhaps even more important to the success of the London venture was Stravinsky's open letter to Diaghilev heralding the revival and pointing out its significance for the twin arts of music and dance. It was while the ballet was enjoying its first success, all too short-lived, that Stravinsky conceived the idea of *Mavra,* that charming *opera buffa* celebrating the three Russian artists he most revered — Pushkin, Glinka, and Tchaikovsky.

Le Baiser de la fée was the climax of Stravinsky's evangelistic activities. This ballet, commissioned by Ida Rubinstein for a new company

she was organizing, was planned as a tribute to Tchaikovsky on the
thirty-fifth anniversary of his death, in November 1928. Whether it
was Stravinsky himself or Alexander Benois who first thought of a
ballet based on Tchaikovsky's music, Stravinsky carried out the idea
with enthusiasm. He chose Hans Christian Andersen's fairy tale, *The
Ice Maiden,* as his story. The musical plan was to borrow thematic
material from Tchaikovsky or to invent it in Tchaikovsky's manner,
and to produce the whole in the spirit of Tchaikovsky's great Maryinsky
ballets.

The score bears the following dedication:

Je dédie ce ballet à la mémoire de Pierre Tchaikovsky en apparentant **sa**
Muse à cette fée et c'est en cela que ce ballet devient une allégorie. Cette muse
l'a également marqué de son baiser fatal dont la mystérieuse empreinte se fait
ressentir sur toute l'oeuvre du grand artiste.

IGOR STRAWINSKY
1928

I dedicate this ballet to the memory of Peter Tchaikovsky, identifying his
Muse with the fairy. The ballet thus becomes an allegory. This Muse similarly
branded him with her fatal kiss, whose mysterious imprint made itself felt in all
the work of this great artist.

The dedication does not make the allegory at all clear. It suggests an
analogy between the kiss bestowed on the infant by the Fairy (first
scene of the ballet) and the Muse's gift of genius to Tchaikovsky. But
in the course of the ballet it turns out that the Alpine Fairy is malign —
there is something of Carabosse in her, and of Odile too. Her fatal kiss
marked the infant not for a life of fulfilled promise and happiness but
for an early death. By the second scene the infant has become the
handsome Young Man ready for the joys of marriage. But the Fairy
snatches him from his Fiancée on their wedding day and drags him
down into the icy Alpine lake to a life of eternal bliss. Eternal though
this bliss may be, it surely is not the kind of bliss that men have ever
hoped for in either this life or the next. By all human standards (for
which the writers of fairy tales have often found the most inhuman
substitutes), the Fairy's kiss is not a blessing at all, but a curse. Alle-
gorically, then, we should expect Tchaikovsky's muse to be as malign
as the Fairy of the ballet. Indeed, was she not? Was it not her fatal
kiss that accounts for almost everything from the sexual tragedy of
Tchaikovsky's life to the vulgarity of his symphonic climaxes and his
boring sequences?

All this adds up to a very small point, to be sure, but the ambiguity of Stravinsky's dedicatory paragraph might well be taken as a reflection of an ambivalent attitude towards Tchaikovsky. At the very most, Stravinsky loves Tchaikovsky in spite of unforgivable faults. It is a love that is willed rather than inspired, a love *faute de mieux*. What Russian composer is there whom a Stravinsky could idealize? Thus it happens that the "great artist" of the dedication has very little greatness and still less artistry in the score of *Le Baiser de la fée*. All the virtues there are Stravinsky's.

One must look at the score, then, and not at the dedication, to find out precisely what Stravinsky's attitude towards Tchaikovsky is. At the present, fourteen pieces (all of them for piano or for voice with piano accompaniment) can be cited positively as major source material. In addition, there are many references, some of them hardly more than metaphorical, to other works. Some of the borrowings are so disguised as to elude identification, and they leave the researcher confident that others must have escaped him altogether. Stravinsky himself is of no help here. Under Robert Craft's persistent questioning, he forced his memory to offer up six or seven "correct attributions."[1] But all of these are not correct and they do not include all that Craft himself listed in his notes for Stravinsky's recording in 1955.[2] Schaeffner's statement, that all of the melodic material is Tchaikovsky's except the theme accompanying the pursuit of the Mother by the Fairy's retinue (section 14)[3] has never been demonstrated, nor can it be by this writer. Schaeffner had his information from Stravinsky himself when the music was still fresh in his mind, and it must therefore be taken seriously even if it can no longer be quite believed. On the other hand, the composer now says that he cannot remember "which music is Tchaikovsky's and which mine."

Let us look at these fourteen works in the order of their appearance in *Le Baiser*. The first of them is the well-known song, *Berceuse de la tempête*,[4] Opus 54, No. 10. The ballet opens with preludings on

---

[1] Stravinsky and Robert Craft, *Expositions and Developments*, Garden City, N. Y., 1962, pp. 73-75. Unless otherwise noted, all statements attributed to Stravinsky are from this source.

[2] Columbia Masterworks ML 5102.

[3] André Schaeffner, *Strawinsky*, Paris, 1931, p. 116.

[4] Since the titles used by American and English publishers are so varied, I prefer to use the French, which are far more consistent. Besides, many Russian publishers, especially Jurgenson, printed their title pages in both Russian and French. All of Stravinsky's Russian works, beginning with *L'Oiseau de feu*, had bilingual title pages. I retain the French and, in all other instances, the language of the original edition.

the theme, and the whole of the melody, with some development, accompanies the beginning of Tableau I, the scene of the Mother lulling her child in the midst of the storm. Stravinsky does not adhere strictly to Tchaikovsky's harmony, and of course the orchestral conception is entirely Stravinsky's. But there is nothing out of character with the original — the treatment must be judged loving and respectful but also imaginative. The song recurs interestingly at the end of the scene (section 40), but more importantly in the final scene, where the Fairy slowly drags the Young Man to watery bliss. After a few measures of introduction, the melody is presented in a telescoped version and with a thoroughly Stravinskian accompaniment. From here to the end, the music is entirely Stravinsky's — one of his most beautiful examples of attenuated, silent music. Tchaikovskian elements are present but they no longer bear any significant relation to their origin. The melody of the *Berceuse* continues, but in the major mode. For counterpoint there is a theme for horn which Stravinsky now thinks he may have borrowed. Its source remains obscure. Most curious is the accompaniment figure. It is merely present at the beginning of the scene, gradually gaining in importance and finally becoming the basic substance of the music. In the growing· process (at section 222) its intervals take on a configuration familiar but almost hidden in the slow tempo and *ostinato* rhythm:

Ex. 1

This association of *Le Baiser* with the Scherzo of Symphony No. 6 may indeed be a descent into mere tune detection; and yet, as will be seen later, the mysteries of *Le Baiser* require just this kind of scrutiny.

In the long D-minor *Allegro sostenuto* that comprises the bulk of Tableau I, there is only one theme that can positively be identified as Tchaikovsky's. It is the piano interlude separating the stanzas of the song, *Soir d'hiver*, Opus 54, No. 7. It makes four appearances, the first of them at section 13:2-7.

Ex. 2

In each appearance the Tchaikovsky theme is referred to, not quoted verbatim. The two longer references vary the original enough to be called developments. But the most interesting development is saved for the coda of the scene, Vivace, at section 42. Here the basic motif is harped on for seven measures; suddenly, by inversion and transposition, it becomes a new idea altogether (section 43):

Ex. 3

The constructive intervals (semitone, sixth, and the latter's inversion) comprise practically the whole of the melodic material for the coda; the bass line is limited almost completely to chromatic movement, and the whole brilliant passage ends in a spiraling chromaticism.

For the village music of Tableau II Stravinsky picks a whole bouquet of bucolic themes from Tchaikovsky's piano music, stringing them together on a chain of two ideas from the familiar *Humoresque*, Opus 10, No. 2. The piece is too well known to require quotation here — everyone knows how it sounds on the piano and ought to be able to recognize that the commercial, potted-palm orchestrations are literal translations that merely assign notes to convenient instruments. Stravinsky's translation for brass instruments, and with transposition to D major, is a brilliant and witty discovery. It can well bear the repetition it gets during the scene, for, unlike the original, it is constantly refreshed by new juxtapositions of its phrases, subtle changes of **har-mony**, varying instrumentation, and a few counterpoints the **most** amusing of which is a direct quote (for violins and 'cellos at section 61) of one of Tchaikovsky's "winding-up" figures from the Finale of Symphony No. 4 (measures 111-118). *Humoresque*'s downward-leaping ninth in the bass, a mere habit in Tchaikovsky's scheme, becomes useful to Stravinsky in new contexts throughout the scene.

The introduction of the *Humoresque* motifs (Stravinsky presents them in reverse order) is interrupted by some quiet music borrowed from the opening of *Rêverie du soir*, Opus 19, No. 1. Tchaikovsky had composed a dialogue for the two hands, with regular two-measure phrases duly repeated, the chain of sequences proceeding unruffled. Stravinsky recomposes the material, making use of the melodic motifs and the harmony but giving them a fresh rhythmical shape, eliminating the routine figures in sixteenth notes, avoiding exact repetition, and casting the whole for the medium of a solo string quartet. Stravinsky has forgotten his source for this music—he calls it "my development," which it surely is, and far more interesting than the original. His term for the whole introduction to the scene is "my *Bearbeitung.*"

When the curtain rises on this scene, he continues with the middle section of the *Rêverie du soir*. This is another translation from piano to brass:

Ex. 4

The transformation is rather drastic, for Stravinsky's *mf pesante* is quite the opposite of the gentle rhythmic pulse of the original. His metaphor is obviously that of two accordions playing in contrary motion, as in

Scherzo à la russe twenty years later. It is undoubtedly the metaphor that led Stravinsky to misremember this music as *Le Paysan joue à l'accordéon,* Opus 39, No. 12. This amusing little piece (it consists of a single three-measure theme, Adagio, repeated over and over again) does actually occur as a counterpoint to the *Humoresque* a little later, at section 64:5 and again in sections 76-77. In order to accommodate its shape, Stravinsky is obliged to invent a new phrasing for the *Humoresque* theme — another stroke of wit that will be missed if one listens only to the trombone echo of *Le Paysan* or the yodeling by piccolo and flutes. This little passage is a delightful and thoroughly un-Tchaikovskian quodlibet:

Ex. 5

One of Stravinsky's less familiar sources, which he himself has completely forgotten, is Tchaikovsky's piano piece, *Au village,* Opus 40, No. 7. The second strain of the middle section, *Allegro molto vivace,* is lifted out of obscurity for the E-major dance of the village scene (section 70). A mildly amusing polka in the original, it becomes a *grotesquerie* in Stravinsky's treatment. Changes of instrumental timbre break up the opening phrase into tiny segments; then a few notes of the melody are "soured," a comic canonic imitation is introduced briefly, and the 2/4 meter of the tune is miswed to a 3/8 accompaniment. Later, at section 87, the *mésalliance* is reversed — a 3/8 tune with a 2/4 accompaniment. Here it is part of the waltz movement that begins at section 78 with the well known *Natha-Valse,* Opus 51, No. 4, and continues with waltz versions of all the previous melodies.

With the dispersion of the village crowd on stage, Stravinsky returns to his drama. The entrance of the Fairy, now disguised as a

Gypsy, is signalled by some forty measures (sections 97-101) of quiet
music taken from the opening of *Au village,* terminating in harmonies
that echo through from the first scene (section 12:5-6). This whole
passage is made up of typically Tchaikovskian sequences with the sym-
metries only slightly disturbed — but still disturbed. The Gypsy now
begins to work her magic charms on the Young Man, but what eventually happens to him is less surprising than the changes wrought by
Stravinsky on Tchaikovsky's very Schumannesque song, *Tant triste,
tant douce,* Opus 6, No. 3. Here is the pertinent portion of the original
melody with a reduced accompaniment:

Ex. 6

This is another of the pieces that Stravinsky can no longer recall. Small
wonder, for he recomposed it so completely that it is in fact his own.
Transposition to A minor is the principal alteration, for it changes the
whole character of the music from the warm, tender, and passionate
voice of a lover to the insidiously enchanting dance of a gypsy. Stravinsky's recomposition of the song is best shown not at the beginning of the
dance, where he deals with motifs, but later (section 106:2), where his
version of the whole melody makes comparison possible. It is given here
in his own piano reduction:

Ex. 7

The two measures under the bracket are worth examining for a moment, for they throw some light on the possible origin of a strikingly Tchaikovskian but unidentifiable melody that appears in the introduction to the first scene of the ballet and is subsequently developed in the D-minor Allegro of that scene. Illustration serves better than description:

Ex. 8

Certainly this is tune-detection. Still, Symphony No. 5 is very present in Stravinsky's thoughts: a little later in the Gypsy dance, at section 113, there is a direct quotation of the same phrase from the symphony, very plain in the first violins but with competition from counterpoints in the winds.

Ex. 9

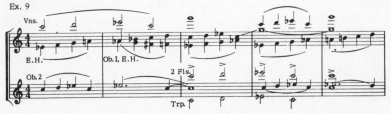

Also, in the same section of the dance (110), the bass line is at least an echo, if not a conscious borrowing of the bass in the finale of Symphony No. 5 (measure 128 ff.). Is this mere coincidence? It is difficult to believe, for *Le Baiser* is rich in references of this sort, indispensable to the evocation of Tchaikovsky's style.

Tableau III is a ballet suite consisting of an introduction, a dance for the women of the corps de ballet, and a classical *pas de deux* having an *Entrée* for the Young Man, an Adagio for him and his Fiancée, a Variation for her, and a Coda. For the introduction Stravinsky borrows two ideas from the central section of *Scherzo humoristique,* Opus 19, No. 2: an inverted pedal on the dominant with pretty chords below it, and a broad melody. This time there is nothing cabalistic in Stravinsky's treatment of the material, though he enriches all of it both harmonically and contrapuntally. The music for the corps de ballet is in classical dance form. The principal theme is the beginning part of *Scherzo humoristique,*[5] transformed from triple to duple meter and having a phrase-length of nine measures. The secondary theme is the B-minor section of *Feuillet d'album,* Opus 19, No. 3, with its two-measure phrase extended to five.[6] The beginning of the same piece provides the trio of Stravinsky's dance.

The *Pas de deux* begins with the entry of the Young Man, for which Stravinsky recasts the middle part of the Nocturne, Opus 19, No. 4.

Ex. 10

Stravinsky calls this "my imitation of the famous variation in *The Sleeping Beauty*." This again is probably a slip of the memory, for if the music resembles anything at all, it is the *Panorama* of that ballet. In spite of its notation, the Young Man's dance sounds like a waltz. Its

---

[5] Stravinsky finds an affinity between this and the scherzo of *Manfred.*

[6] Stravinsky recommends a comparison of this development with his *Orpheus* (section 50). The comparison is interesting. So is a comparison with measure 116, first movement of Symphony No. 5.

second melodic idea, at section 160, has a brief resemblance to the two-measure phrase at the *tranquillo* of *Valse sentimentale,* Opus 51, No. 6, but this is a comparison that perhaps should not be pursued too eagerly.

In the following Adagio, the clarinet arpeggios (section 166) are plainly an imitation of the flute at the beginning of the *Pas de deux* from *The Sleeping Beauty.* But the 'cello melody is one of Stravinsky's most obscure derivations. It comes from a song, *Serenada,* Opus 63, No. 6, originally in G major but transposed here for purposes of illus-

Ex. 11

tration. If this derivation seems not only obscure but even far-fetched, the skeptic must look a little further, where he finds the following:

Ex. 12

It is almost at the end of the Adagio (section 174) that Stravinsky makes a passing reference to measure 25 of the famous *Andante cantabile* of the String Quartet, Opus 11.

The Coda is claimed by Stravinsky as his own music. At least one part of it is not — the tune begun by trombones at section 184, with a counterstatement by trumpets and oboes at 186 and a clinching cheer by the full orchestra at 189. This is the D-major part of *Polka peu dansante,* Opus 51, No. 2. For Tchaikovsky, the tune is to be played *quieto* and *mf* in an *Allegro moderato,* something quite different from Stravinsky's Presto and boisterous delivery. But a cue for the latter reading might have been taken from Tchaikovsky's use of a portion of the same tune in the *Valse de salon,* Opus 51, No. 1. The pertinent passages are too long for quotation here; but if the three be examined together, it will be seen that at least in this instance some of Stravinsky's practices in *Le Baiser* follow his master's example.

The *dénouement* of the drama occurs in the *Scène,* where the Young Man falls completely under the sway of the Fairy and is led away to his felicitous doom. The music is of course Stravinsky's orchestral setting of Tchaikovsky's most famous song, *Ah! qui brûla d'amour* (None but the lonely heart, None but the weary heart, Ye who have yearned alone, etc.), Opus 6, No. 6. Every measure of the two versions should be compared in detail. This is the largest single Tchaikovskian chunk that Stravinsky used for his score, and the only one that required Stravinsky to collaborate in a grand symphonic-operatic climax. His collaboration was wholehearted, one feels. By way of preparation he invented an introduction of fourteen measures, which may perhaps be a little long for a piece having only 60 measures. Still, one would not do without them, for this is now theater, not the concert hall. In the last bars of section 207, and going on into 208, he adds imitative sequences, a Tchaikovskian trait that he has meticulously avoided throughout the score — except where (as here) he can make them unexpected within the formal scheme and unpredictable harmonically. The grand climax is actually longer than Tchaikovsky's, luxuriantly *pathétique* in its harmony, and even hectic in the horn parts. In the context of Stravinsky's whole *oeuvre,* even as it existed in 1928, this is a strange and unique piece. But given the theatrical occasion, and the position of the piece in a forty-five-minute work, it seems as inevitable in its expression as it is masterful in its craft.

With all these materials before us, even though they cannot be adequately displayed here, we might try for some conclusions concerning the Stravinsky-Tchaikovsky relationship. It must be observed first of all that only two Tchaikovsky compositions are used whole — the *Berceuse* and *Ah! qui brûla d'amour.* Yet both are subjected to considerable adjustment in the process of converting them to Stravinsky's use. All the other Tchaikovsky materials are excerpts. Some of them are just barely recognizable, so deeply hidden, so clandestinely derived, or so completely transformed as to leave one wondering why Stravinsky took the trouble to make use of them in the first place. Would not pure invention have been easier? Probably so; but it was not a question of taking trouble or finding an easy way. As a homage to Tchaikovsky, *Le Baiser de la fée* had to be steeped in his music, not only so that there would be an external show of the steeping but so that there would be an internal, even if unperceived, conviction of it. That is why one senses Tchaikovsky's presence even when one cannot point out precisely what makes the presence felt.

At various times, Stravinsky has expressed admiration for Tchaikovsky's gift of melody. Still, it is just this gift with which he seems to be most dissatisfied. With rare exceptions, the melodies are altered — not only their very notes but also their rhythmic structure, tempo, harmony, and, perhaps most important, their contexts. Indeed, Stravinsky treats them as themes rather than melodies (it is *his* distinction that one follows), as materials for development rather than as self-sufficient entities. For him, Tchaikovsky's *oeuvre* is a storehouse of raw material, not unlike a collection of folk music.

This is of course as it should be, for Stravinsky is a composer, not an arranger. If he were the latter, he might have written a Grand Fantasia in the manner of the 19th century, *à la* Liszt, Czerny, Moscheles or Busoni. This was not his intention. He has described his score as "inspired by the music of Tchaikovsky," and this is precisely what it is. For inspiration he needed melodies less than ideas, and he needed ideas that he could make his own through the working of his own syntax, idiom, accent, craft.

He was inspired also, but in a more general way, by Tchaikovsky's elegance, humor, and broadly universal rather than narrowly nationalistic orientation. Inspired, but not necessarily influenced, for these were qualities that he possessed inherently and shared with, rather than owed to, Tchaikovsky. With so much in common, it was not difficult to fuse his own with Tchaikovsky's personality — or rather, to absorb it. For in the end, *Le Baiser* is more Stravinsky's than Tchaikovsky's. What reminds the listener of Tchaikovsky is the tunes (where they are recognizable), plus the metaphorical references, plus the distillation of certain stylistic traits. What convinces the listener of Stravinsky is the total music. Stravinsky's hand shows everywhere, and it is the ruling hand, the hand that chooses and disposes. Some "impurity" appears just when things seem to be going along in the most purely Tchaikovskian vein — some twist of harmony, rhythm, or orchestration. Sequences, the bane of Tchaikovskian form, abound; but instead of being Tchaikovsky's inevitable squares they are Stravinsky's rhomboids, scalenes, trapeziums, or trapezoids — shapes somehow stretched or shrunken into asymmetry and arranged in unpredictable combinations. Tchaikovsky's faults — his banalities and vulgarities and routine procedures — are composed *out* of the music, and Stravinsky's virtues are composed *into* it. Everywhere, Stravinsky invoked Tchaikovsky; everywhere he composed his own music.

Le Baiser de la fée is thus an act of criticism, criticism at its most rigorous. As a portrait of Tchaikovsky, it is no likeness at all, as that of Pergolesi was. As an act of homage, it is surely one of the most curious ever conceived by one composer for another. Stravinsky closes his eyes — his ears, rather — to Tchaikovsky's faults; and he corrects his virtues. Necessarily, he ignores the bulk of the music. For there is actually very little of which he can approve. The familiar image of the iceberg is useful here: the bulk of the work is submerged, and what appears above water is but a fraction of the whole. Even here, in the two categories to which Stravinsky limited his borrowings, there is not much acceptable music. When one goes through the complete piano music (a hundred-odd pieces) and the complete songs (another hundred), he sees how these works enlarge the figure of the tragic symphonist, the lachrymose sentimentalist — and, let it be said, the hack composer. Had Stravinsky been obliged to mine more gold in the mountain of Tchaikovsky's piano and vocal compositions, he would not have had many strikes.

Of course Stravinsky is aware of this. But at a certain moment of his career he needed the figure of Tchaikovsky as a symbol of Russian music from which he himself stemmed, to which he has always remained umbilical. He has recreated Tchaikovsky not in his own image but in the image of the distinguished figure that the twelve-year-old Igor once glimpsed in the foyer of the Maryinsky Theater.

STRAVINSKY'S CONCEPT
OF VARIATIONS

By ROBERT U. NELSON

I N writing variations my method is to remain faithful to the theme
as a *melody* — never mind the rest!" Thus Igor Stravinsky described
to me over a decade ago the essence of his variation technique. "I
regard the theme as a melodic skeleton," he continued, "and am very
strict in exposing it in the variations. As in writing a fugue, I am faithful
to the —" Here, instead of finishing the sentence, he briskly stepped off
an imaginary theme on the floor of his library — two vigorous paces
ahead, one to the right, two to the rear — and ended his illustration,
cadence-like, with a smart military salute. His meaning was unmistakable. Stravinsky's concept of variations, like his idea of music as a whole,
is that of a disciplined and logical art. Technically it embraces two
divergent attitudes: faithful adherence to the melody of the theme,
unlimited freedom in handling the other thematic elements.

Stravinsky's variation sets are invariably movements in larger works.
The earliest appears in *Pulcinella* (1919); the others are found in the
Octet for Wind Instruments (1922-23), the Concerto for Two Pianos
(1935), *Jeu de cartes* (1936), *Danses concertantes* (1941-42), the
Sonata for Two Pianos (1943-44), the *Ebony Concerto* (1945), and the
Septet (1953).[1]

The *Pulcinella* variations are in a class apart, since they are but
adaptations of the originals attributed to Pergolesi, but beginning with
the "Tema con variazioni" movement of the Octet Stravinsky's char-

[1] The division of the movements into separate variations is indicated in all
scores except the Octet, the *Ebony Concerto,* and the Septet. In the Octet the
division is: theme, no. 24; var. 1, no. 26; var. 2, no. 28; var. 3, no. 31; var. 4,
no. 33; var. 5, no. 38; var. 6, no. 49; var. 7, no. 51.

In the *Ebony Concerto* the division is: theme, p. 21; var. 1, no. 3; var. 2,
no. 21; var. 3, no. 24; coda, no. 33.

In the Septet the division is: theme, up-beat to measure 1; var. 1, m. 8;
var. 2, m. 16; var. 3, m. 24; var. 4, m. 32; var. 5, m. 40; var. 6, m. 48; var. 7,
m. 56; var. 8, m. 64; var. 9, m. 72.

acteristic technique emerges. Here are found the sharp contrasts of mood
that mark the later sets almost without exception; here also are seen
those prevailingly wide departures from the theme's formal design that
signalize the free-variation technique, his favorite method. Within the
Octet as a whole the somber theme and seven diverse variations act as
the slow movement, thus establishing another precedent observed in most
later works. In the "Quattro variazioni" of the Concerto for Two
Pianos we encounter greater suavity coupled with an abundance of
ostinato elements, and manifold patterns of figuration which are at times
elegantly ornate, at others vigorous. The five variations and coda contained in the ballet, *Jeu de cartes,* midway in the "Deuxième donne,"
are prevailingly light and graceful, touched by a quiet romanticism. In
Danses concertantes, written for small orchestra, the lengthy theme and
four spacious variations of the "Thème varié" provide a relaxed, thin-
textured contrast to the Baroque-like mass and animation of the first
two movements. The straightforward, occasionally contrapuntal Largo
of the Sonata for Two Pianos shows a different approach. Departing
from his customary emphasis upon the free-variation technique, Stravinsky here writes variations that are prevailingly structural, following
closely the formal plan of the slow-moving theme in three out of the
four members of the series. In the *Ebony Concerto,* scored for jazz band,
the variations occupy the exceptional position of concluding movement.
Embodying the free technique, the series consists of a simple theme,
three variations, and a short coda. The second-movement Passacaglia of
the Septet is Stravinsky's only use of a ground-bass form, and his only
variations to show serial treatment. Built upon a fragmentary theme that
suggests Webern, the nine structural variations are somber, thick-
textured, and dissonant, and of an extraordinary contrapuntal complexity.

These diverse sets bear out conclusively Stravinsky's own statement
as to his method. The true bond between theme and variations is the
melody of the theme; all other thematic elements are largely ignored.
But — and this is important — when Stravinsky speaks of remaining
"faithful to the theme as a melody" he does not imply a literal adherence, for the degree of contact fluctuates widely, ranging from nearly
exact quotations of the melody to vague suggestions of it through casual
motivic allusions and developments; from clearly recognizable expansions, in which the melody is presented piecemeal, spun out by motivic
extensions, to the most venturesome and at times ambiguous transformations. Often the "melodic skeleton" that he is "very strict in exposing

. . . in the variations" is used so freely as to become simply an abstract succession of pitch names (like the D, E, B, C♯, D succession in the Concerto for Two Pianos, where D stands for any D, E for any E, and so on), with the result that the original contour is generally altered profoundly. In other words, Stravinsky's adherence to the chosen line is occasionally close but more often tenuous, marked by the abandonment of its formal design and melodic individuality.

The themes upon which Stravinsky builds his variations are notably dissimilar. In length they range from single motifs and phrases (*Jeu de cartes,* Concerto for Two Pianos, Sonata for Two Pianos) to the elaborate tripartite design of *Danses concertantes.* There are strong contrasts of mood: the graceful theme of *Jeu de cartes,* the dark Octet theme, the more conventionally melodious subjects of the Two-Piano Sonata and *Danses concertantes,* the abstract theme of the Septet. The variations of the Two-Piano Concerto are built upon a double theme, thus carrying on a practice as old as Haydn's Variations in F minor; Stravinsky believes that the use of two contrasting thematic ideas gives a composer "opportunity for greater scope in the variations."[2] Normally Stravinsky states his theme before the first variation, but in *Jeu de cartes* and the Two-Piano Concerto he begins the variations without prior thematic announcement. The element of repetition is strong; one thinks at once of the restrictive, intentionally monotonous themes of the Octet and *Ebony Concerto*; of *Danses concertantes,* where the theme itself is almost a variation because of its many repetitive extensions; and of the curiously redundant subject of the Two-Piano Sonata, restated three times before the first variation begins.

Stravinsky's closest approach to a literal use of the melodic subject comes in the Octet, where variations 1, 3, and 6 — all nearly identical to one another — follow the melody quite exactly; also in the much later Septet, where the passacaglia variations are built on more divergent but still clearly recognizable forms of the original theme.[3] In both sets Stravinsky's developmental method is to decorate the thematic line by

[2] The two contrasting ideas of the Concerto theme are the subject of the fourth-movement fugue, quoted in its entirety in Ex. 10a; and the melodic fragment in mm. 6-8 of the *Preludio* (E, G, A, C, D, G). The theme of *Danses concertantes* likewise contains two contrasting motifs, although to apply the term double theme would scarcely be accurate here; the first motif (part A of the theme) begins at no. 64, the second (part B of the theme) begins one beat after no. 68.

[3] Another example, the completely literal quotation of the melodic subject in the second variation of the *Ebony Concerto,* is not pertinent to the discussion, since there Stravinsky's purpose is a thematic *da capo* rather than a variation in the developmental sense.

adding figurations and counterpoints in the remaining voices. Thus at
the outset of the three similar Octet variations, and again towards their
close, the melodic subject is presented quite literally and broadly in the
trombones, while the remaining instruments engage in a swirling figuration above (Ex. 1). The prototype of this idea is the *cantus firmus*

variation of the 16th to 18th centuries, of which William Byrd's *John
come kisse me now* and Samuel Scheidt's *Christe, qui lux es et dies* are
examples.[4] But Stravinsky's handling differs noticeably from that of the
earlier composers in his transposition of the melody to different keys
(shown in Ex. 1, where the melodic subject in variation 1 begins D, B♭, D
instead of C♯, A, C♯ as in the theme) and in his occasional transformations (as in measures 5 to 7 of variation 1, where a portion of the
melody is presented in crisply syncopated form against a rapid *ostinato*
pattern in the bassoons). Moreover, the way in which Stravinsky tele-
scopes the melody at the close of variation 1 is without precedent in the
early *cantus firmus* variation (Ex. 2).

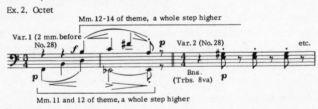

The additions of counterpoints to the principal line of the theme
is even more conspicuous in the passacaglia of the Septet. The theme is
presented in the bass, once during each variation, much altered through
octave transpositions; but because the original row-form of the sixteen-
tone series, and the rhythms of its initial presentation, are maintained
during these restatements the theme's identity is never in doubt.[5] Above

    [4] For a discussion of these and other early pieces see Robert U. Nelson, *The
Technique of Variation,* Berkeley and Los Angeles, 1948, pp. 34-41, 57-62.
    [5] The row is E, B, A, G, F♯, G♯, C♯, B, G, F♯, G♯, G, A, C, G♯, A. For an
important analysis of the Septet, especially detailed in its discussion of the passacaglia movement, see Erwin Stein, *Strawinsky's Septet (1953),* in *Tempo,* 31
(Spring 1954), 7-10.

the bass Stravinsky adds rhythmically free canons at various intervals of imitation; built on different row forms and transpositions, two or more of the canons usually proceed simultaneously. The resulting texture, suggested in Example 3, once more recalls the early *cantus firmus* variation, especially the elaborate canonic construction of Bach's *Vom Himmel hoch, da komm' ich her.*[6]

Ex. 3. Septet (1953)

More common than the relatively close thematic quoting just described is Stravinsky's development of thematic motifs. This technique appears in the Octet (variations 2, 5, and 7), *Danses concertantes* (variation 4), the Sonata for Two Pianos (variation 3), the *Ebony Concerto* (variation 1), and most conspicuously of all in *Jeu de cartes,* where it is the ruling method throughout. In his use of motivic development Stravinsky again follows an old tradition within the variation form, one that became firmly established during the 19th century, at first in the character variations of Beethoven, Schumann, and Brahms, later in free variations by Franck, d'Indy, Elgar, and their contemporaries. These composers generally altered their thematic figures, sometimes drastically, before using them in the variations. Exceptionally, Stravinsky follows this method of marked alteration, as in the fifth variation of *Jeu de cartes* (Ex. 4). But as a rule he establishes a much

Ex. 4. *Jeu de cartes* (1936)

[6] This work was transcribed by Stravinsky in 1955 for choir and orchestra.

plainer connection, like that in Examples 6 to 8. His manipulation of the motifs is, in the main, rather rudimentary. There is little contrapuntal handling; often the development consists only in spinning out the motif by means of repetition or sequence, as in Example 5.

Ex. 5. *Jeu de cartes*

Stravinsky's chief use of motivic development is in combination with intrinsic expansions of the complete theme: short developments, acting as extensions, are interpolated between successive portions of the theme, thereby drawing it out. One sees the method with particular clarity in the first variation of the *Ebony Concerto* (Ex. 6), where the theme is lengthened by varied repetitions of syncopated thematic figures. Here

Ex. 6. *Ebony Concerto* (1945)

the subject is carried into the variation without significant change, save for the extensions. Often the presence of the theme is less readily apparent, as in the excerpt from *Danses concertantes* (Ex. 7); here one finds the same technique of expansion but in connection with marked trans-

Ex. 7. *Danses concertantes* (1941-42)

formations, not only of single motifs but also of the theme as a whole. As before, the repetitive element is strong. In the quotation from the Octet (Ex. 8) the theme is still further disguised — so completely,

Ex. 8. Octet

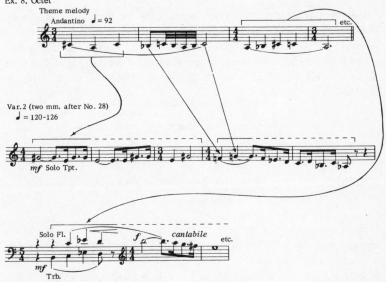

indeed, that one is only certain of its presence after careful scrutiny. The underlying method is again the spinning-out of the subject through motivic extensions. Thus in Examples 6, 7, and 8 we see the same basic construction but an increasing concealment of the theme. Stravinsky's manner of expanding a theme through motivic extensions may be traced to an occasional prior use in Baroque chorale variations. Incongruous as it may seem, there is a similarity of method between Bach's organ partita, *Christ, der du bist der helle Tag,* and the variation movement in the *Ebony Concerto,* written over two centuries later for the modern dance orchestra.[7]

[7] See especially the opening variations of these works. In the Stravinsky movement, as in the Bach chorale variations, the amplified theme is often combined with *ostinato*-like figures in other voices. For Bach's treatment see Nelson, *op. cit.,* pp. 62-64.

Even more important than the development of motifs in Stravinsky's variations is the allied device of theme transformation. This technique, involving the conspicuous alteration of a large part of the theme, or even of the theme as a whole, first became prominent in the variation form at the close of the 19th century, coincident with the rise of the free variation; since that time few composers of free variations have done without it. Yet even where Stravinsky follows precedent he refuses to be orthodox, and so it is not surprising that his theme transformations exhibit a degree of change rarely shown by earlier variation writers.

As used in the variation form, theme transformation generally means that however much a melody is altered in rhythm, tone color, dynamics, tempo, and the like, its contour remains largely unchanged. Stravinsky occasionally transforms themes in this traditional manner, as in Example 9, an excerpt from the Two-Piano Sonata. Here the contour of the

Ex. 9. Two-Piano Sonata (1943-44)

melodic subject is plainly kept in spite of the faster tempo, the lower register, and the more nervous rhythm; and even though the interval of a third has become a tenth, the fourth an eleventh, and so on. But he usually forsakes the contour of the melodic subject along with its other characteristics, retaining only its succession of pitch names. Thus, in the first variation of the Concerto for Two Pianos (Ex. 10a), the original thematic line is often barely recognizable; for not only has its rhythmic vigor given way to an undulating, gently syncopated movement, but in addition there has come a new melodic configuration through the changing of intervals — a descending fourth (E, B) becoming a rising fifth, an ascending second (B, C♯) becoming a falling seventh, and so on. In other words, Stravinsky transposes a majority of his theme tones either an octave or two octaves from their original locations, and does this irregularly, shifting some tones upward, some downward. The multiformity of contours achieved through this means becomes increasingly apparent in the next two variations, each of which is in a different key (Ex. 10b, c). The lines in all three are so individualized that at first

glance they appear totally unrelated, yet the derivation of each from a
common source is actually very strict.[8]

Ex. 10. Two-Piano Concerto (1935)

a. Var. 1 (m. 2)

b. Var. 2

c. Var. 3 (m. 3)

Composers have used octave transpositions to disguise the melodic
contour of themes for centuries, but in a manner that was incidental and
casual compared with Stravinsky's more thoroughgoing procedure. As
early as Wolfgang Ebner's *36 Variations on an Air,* a typical 17th-
century structural series, octave transpositions were used occasionally as
part of a general embellishing process;[9] most later composers of structural
variations have employed them with equal reserve. Even in the com-
paratively recent free variation, with its emphasis upon theme transformation, the use of octave transpositions has been rare in relation to other
changes. But in Stravinsky's Octet variations, and still more in those of

[8] A similar approach has already been seen in the Septet (Ex. 3), where the
passacaglia theme is much altered in contour by octave displacements.

[9] Nelson, *op. cit.,* p. 43 f.

the Two-Piano Concerto, *Danses concertantes,* the Two-Piano **Sonata,** and the Septet, these transpositions are a commonplace. Here the idea of the melodic subject as contour, as line, often has no meaning.

The beginning of this peculiarly 20th-century kind of theme transformation cannot be credited to Stravinsky alone, for a concurrent impulse is observable in the early Schoenberg school. Antedating slightly Stravinsky's first use in the Octet variations of 1922-1923 is a significant example in Berg's opera, *Wozzeck,* completed in 1921: the remarkable first-act passacaglia, built upon a twelve-tone theme that later is fragmented and freely dispersed among various octaves. Another important manifestation, contemporaneous with the Octet, appears in the serially constructed variation movement of Schoenberg's Serenade, completed in 1923, where again the theme is freely altered through octave displacements. The chance that Stravinsky may have known of these parallel developments prior to his writing of the Octet seems remote, since the Serenade was not published until 1924 and the first production of *Wozzeck* took place in 1925. More probably the radically changed lines were introduced independently by Stravinsky on the one hand, and by Berg and Schoenberg on the other. Whether or not a causal relation exists, the similarity of melodic result is striking, the wide-intervalled lines of the Stravinsky variations often resembling the angular configurations of the early atonal and serial composers. This angularity, already observed in the Concerto for Two Pianos (Ex. 10), is also prominent in *Danses concertantes* (Ex. 11a), in the Sonata for Two Pianos (Ex. 11b), and of course in the Septet, where Stravinsky himself adopts the serial method.

Ex. 11

a. *Danses concertantes,* Var. 1

b. Two-Piano Sonata, Var. 2, m. 31

Stravinsky's disposition of these strikingly transformed lines within the separate variations follows no single plan. Sometimes a theme appears once or twice in its entirety, as in the Sonata for Two Pianos, variations 1, 2, and 4. More generally, a transformed fragment, rather than the entire theme, forms the basis for a variation, as in the fourth variation of the Octet. Occasionally, as in variation 4 of *Danses concertantes,* transformed theme fragments alternate with sections of motivic development. The variations in the Concerto for Two Pianos, built upon a double theme, show a consistent alternation of the two component motifs, with the motifs sometimes complete, sometimes incomplete.[10] The fourth of the Concerto variations has a particularly novel plan, original with Stravinsky, wherein a transformed fragment of the first motif is repeated intermittently throughout in the manner of an *ostinato* (Ex. 12); this unusual method recurs in the first and third variations of *Danses concertantes.* Two fugal treatments — one in the Octet, variation 7, the

Ex. 12. Two-Piano Concerto
Var. 4 (m. 4)

other in the Sonata for Two Pianos, variation 3 — display still another use of transformed theme fragments. The fugal Octet variation is especially remarkable for its surprises: the ingeniously disguised theme, seemingly so unpromising as a fugue subject; the unearthly sound of the fugue as a whole, with its unconventional plan (the theme is heard only four times) and its emphasis upon slow-moving harmonic masses.

Stravinsky's combining of the separate variations of a series to make an integrated whole is mainly conventional, but not completely so. His controlling purpose is to secure strong contrasts in mood between successive variations, such as are found in 19th-century character variations like Beethoven's *Diabelli* set and Schumann's *Symphonic Etudes;* to this end, he juxtaposes quietness and energy, and contrasts flowing lines with restless articulations. The opposition between the successive members of a series is further heightened by clearly marked final cadences, especially beginning with *Danses concertantes*; and even more by contrasts in key. Some of these key contrasts have few prototypes in earlier variations. Thus in the first four variations of *Jeu de cartes* we find the somewhat

[10] The brilliant second variation, for example, has this plan of˙entries:
    Motif 1 in B-flat (mm. 1-9, piano I)
    Motif 1 (incomplete) in B (mm. 10-12, piano II)
    Motif 2 in G (mm. 12-14, piano II)
    Motif 1 (incomplete) in B-flat (mm. 15-18, both pianos)
    Motif 2 in C-sharp (mm. 20-end, piano II)

novel plan of keys arranged in descending semitones (B-flat, A, A-flat, G, followed by a fifth variation in C minor and a coda in G). A similar arrangement, but with the keys ascending, appears in *Danses concertantes* (theme in G, followed by variations in A-flat, A, A, and B-flat). Each of the foregoing sets begins and ends in a different key, probably as the result of broad considerations of tonality involving neighboring movements. This unusual construction is rather general with Stravinsky; only the variations of the Two-Piano Sonata and the *Ebony Concerto* begin and end in the same key. A further idiosyncrasy is the occasional confining of a series to two or three keys used in alternation. Such a restriction may be seen in the Two-Piano Sonata, where the alternating keys are G and D. It may also be found in the Octet, where the emphasis is successively on D, on combinations of D and E, and on A.[11] Here the similarity of variations 1, 3, and 6 — all of which have the same key plan — contributes to a rondo effect. The idea of mixing variations with rondo is an old one, familiar since the 17th century. Stravinsky again suggests this hybrid form in the *Ebony Concerto* and the Septet, but in these later sets he maintains a single tonality throughout.[12]

These rondo-like recurrences, and the other repetitive constructions already discussed, suggest the importance of the repetitive aspect in Stravinsky's variations. Indeed, the repetitive element is in a sense a cornerstone of his method. It shows itself not only in recurrences of entire variations, such as those just mentioned, but also in the fashioning of themes, in the repetition of motifs, and in restatements of larger theme fragments. All these manifestations we have seen. One further kind of repetition is perhaps the most significant of all: repetitive figuration. This appears in all sets, in some rather frequently, functioning as an animated background for transformed themes or more literal thematic quotations. Such figuration assumes many forms: repeated chords, as in Example 13a; figures that simulate *ostinati,* as in Example 13b (these are the most common); true *ostinati,* as in Example 13c.

An examination of Stravinsky's many-sided variation art, with all its richness of conception and subtle craftsmanship, leads to a clearer idea of his significance as a variation writer. Plainly his contribution does not lie in the creation of new approaches, for the techniques of

---

[11] The theme is in D; variations 1, 3, and 6 begin in D but end in E; conversely, variation 2 begins in E but ends in D. The remaining variations (4, 5, 7) are in A.

[12] In the *Ebony Concerto* the theme returns as variation 2; in the Septet variations 1, 4, and 7 resemble each other.

Ex. 13

a. *Jeu de cartes*, Var. 1

b. *Ebony Concerto*, Var. 1 (No. 3)

c. Two-Piano Sonata, Var. 1

adding counterpoints, of developing motifs, and of transforming themes existed long before Stravinsky's appropriation of them. His legacy consists, rather, in his innovations of detail, in the freshness with which he has used the old techniques — modifying here, giving a new emphasis there. In no sense is his treatment perfunctory; instead one finds new problems posed and solved in each successive series. This progressive aspect of his music is well known. Stravinsky himself has said, "I never return — I only continue."[13] His attitude is of particular interest in the field of the variation, for here, perhaps more than with other forms, composers have sometimes found it easy to be perfunctory and to "return."[14]

[13] Ingolf Dahl, *Stravinsky in 1946*, in *Modern Music*, XXIII (Summer 1946), 159.

[14] I am greatly indebted to Igor Stravinsky for his generous help in discussing with me his compositions in variation form.

STRAVINSKY IN SOVIET
RUSSIAN CRITICISM

By BORIS SCHWARZ

T HE latest Soviet textbook on the history of Russian music[1] closes with a chapter on Stravinsky. Yet he is virtually ignored in the official *History of Soviet Russian Music*.[2] The implications are clear: Stravinsky has a place in the musical culture of prerevolutionary Russia, but he is excluded from the Soviet era.

This exclusion, however, does not make him immune to criticism. Soviet evaluations of Stravinsky range from wholehearted approval in the 1920s through cautious reappraisal in the 1930s to rigid rejection in the 1940s and 1950s. But Soviet critical opinion transcends the judgment of an individual critic: at all times it is a collective reflection of Soviet esthetic views. As the concept of Socialist Realism emerged in the 1930s, the antagonism to Stravinsky and Western-style modernism grew ever more pronounced. His works continued to be discussed, though in a curious atmosphere of unreality, since they remained unperformed.

This situation has changed somewhat in the last few years. Recorded performances of Stravinsky's late works are made available to the professional members of the Composers' Union; visiting orchestras have played some of his less controversial pieces; and Soviet orchestras are showing renewed interest in his earlier compositions. The critical reaction is as yet divided. After a recent successful performance of Stravinsky's *Symphonies for Wind Instruments* (1920) by the Moscow Philharmonic, one critic asked, "Is it fair that we had to wait forty years to hear this work?"[3] Yet, when in 1959 the New York Philharmonic presented the Piano Concerto (1924) in Moscow it was termed a "manifesto of musical coldness, dryness, and anemia."[4] Stravinsky's forthcoming visit to Soviet

[1] *Istoria Russkoi Muzyki,* ed. N. Tumanina, 3 vols., Moscow, 1957-60.

[2] *Istoria Russkoi Sovietskoi Muzyki,* 3 vols., Moscow, 1956-59.

[3] *Sovietskaya Muzyka,* February 1962, p. 99.

[4] *Sovietskaya Kultura,* Aug. 27, 1959.

Russia will be of great significance, particularly because it will give Soviet audiences the opportunity of hearing his works in authentic performances. What the impact will be, no one can foretell. But before the issues are beclouded by birthday oratory, it might be useful to survey the attitude of Soviet critics towards Stravinsky as it evolved during the past forty-odd years.

*   *

*

Under the tsarist regime, Stravinsky's early "Parisian" ballets — *Firebird* (1910), *Petrushka* (1911), and *Sacre du printemps* (1913) — were known in Russia only through concert performances. After the Revolution of 1917, Stravinsky's works entered the repertory of the reorganized State theaters: *Petrushka* was staged in Leningrad in 1920, *Firebird* in 1921, *Pulcinella* in 1926, *Renard* in 1927. There were also concert performances of *Les Noces* and *Oedipus Rex,* according to Stravinsky's *Autobiography.*[5] His recent remark that his music was performed in Russia "throughout the period of the N.E.P."[6] must not be misunderstood; actually his works were played before, as well as after, the period of the "New Economic Policy," which extended from 1921 to 1928. In the mid-1920s, the composer — who had resided abroad since 1913 — declined an invitation to conduct concerts in Leningrad. Curiously, the invitation was extended by "tovarich Lunacharsky" (as Stravinsky refers to the Commissar of Public Education)[7] who, before the Revolution, had written a none too favorable review of *Sacre du printemps.*[8]

In the artistic life of Soviet Russia the 1920s were a period of bold, often controversial, experimentation, reflecting the tensions within the young state. "You are a revolutionary in music, we are revolutionaries in life. We ought to work together," said Lunacharsky to Prokofiev in 1918.[9] The cause of musical modernism was represented by the Association for Contemporary Music (ACM), which for a brief time was affiliated with the International Society for Contemporary Music. Opposed to the esoteric and cosmopolitan aims of the ACM were various

[5] Stravinsky, *Autobiography,* New York, 1936 (1958), p. 141.

[6] Stravinsky and Robert Craft, *Expositions and Developments,* New York, 1962, p. 55.

[7] *Ibid.*

[8] *Russian Shows in Paris* (1913). Reprinted in A. Lunacharsky, *V Mire Muzyki,* Moscow, 1958.

[9] Serge Prokofiev, *Autobiography, Articles, Reminiscences,* Moscow, c. 1959, p. 50.

"proletarian" musical groups which fought not only Western-style modernism but often also Russian traditionalism. Caught in the middle were the conservative academic circles of the conservatories and institutes who emerged as the ultimate victors.

The most fervent advocate of modern music was the brilliant Boris Asafiev (also known under the pen name Igor Glebov), who was to become the godfather of Soviet musicology. As a historian, Asafiev explored the relationship between Russia's art music and the so-called "oral tradition." His twofold interest in Russianism and Modernism led to his impassioned endorsement of Stravinsky. A few briefer essays on individual works[10] served as preliminary steps for Asafiev's *Book on Stravinsky*,[11] written with enormous verve, courage, and insight. Published in 1929, the book has been out of print for three decades. It is now considered "deeply fallacious" and has been eliminated from all Russian bibliographies on Stravinsky.

Asafiev saw Stravinsky as a cosmopolitan Russian: "Stravinsky is a representative of European urban musical culture . . . But at the same time he is tied to the depth of his soul to Great Russian melos, to folk and peasant songs, vocal as well as instrumental. He carried to the West the rhythms, inflections, and formal principles of Russia's 'music of oral tradition' . . ."[12] Repeatedly, Asafiev criticized the prerevolu-tionary "philistinism": "Stravinsky freed himself quickly from Debussy's Impressionism as well as the domestic Petersburgian-bureaucratic estheticism and chauvinistic academicism which perverted a good harmony book into a 'symbol of faith' . . ."[13] This might be an allusion to Rimsky-Korsakov's textbook, which, since the 1880s, dominated theoretical thought in Russia. In discussing Stravinsky's treatment of folk material, Asafiev contrasted it to the methods of the "Mighty Five" and the "Belayev circle"; quite surprisingly, he compared it to Tchaikovsky's technique:

Stravinsky mastered Russian folk art not as a clever stylist who knows how to conceal the quotations, nor as an ethnographer unable to assimilate the material . . . but as a master of his native language . . .[14] Stravinsky and Tchaikovsky have a common attitude towards folk art: to them it represents living material

[10] I. Glebov, *Zhar Ptitza* (*Firebird;* also on *Petrushka*), Petrograd, 1921. His essay on *Pulcinella* in *I. Stravinsky i evo ballet Pulcinella,* Leningrad, 1925.

[11] B. Asafiev, *Kniga o Stravinskom,* Leningrad, 1929.

[12] *Ibid.,* p. 6.

[13] *Ibid.,* p. 7.

[14] *Ibid.,* p. 7 f.

rather than archaic language suitable only for adaptation and stylization . . .[15] Stravinsky was not afraid to give artistic shape to tunes familiar to everyone while preserving all their characteristic and vital traits . . .[16]

Yet Asafiev realized that Stravinsky's restless spirit was not to be confined to Russian topicality: "Stravinsky became for Europe, and especially for France, what Lully, Gluck, and Cherubini had been before him — great composer-universalists. To us Russians, he has ceased to be a concretely known personality, but his creative work was and remains an outstanding phenomenon . . ."[17]

Stravinsky's "new instrumental style" of the 1920s was not deliberate stylization, or "Bachism," and Asafiev avoids the term "neo-Classical."[18] Yet he felt that Stravinsky had not solved the problem of a new style and had merely created "an artificial language, a musical 'Esperanto,' so to speak . . ." Writing in 1926, Asafiev prophesied that Stravinsky, after having searched for a solution independent of the stage, would "confront the European musician again with an objectively directed, creative synthesis . . . in connection with the theater."[19]

Two years later, Asafiev became acquainted with *Oedipus Rex, Apollon Musagète,* and *Baiser de la fée.* He admired *Oedipus* as the "synthesis of Stravinsky's latest search for a new 'factual' style, not tainted by national or emotional subjectivism."[20] *Apollon* continued the "Europeanization of Stravinsky's musical language," the result being "artificially invented" and having the "worst features of 'Esperanto'."[21] In *Baiser de la fée* Asafiev found more stylistic freshness, but despite the "enchanting" orchestration, Stravinsky's melodic invention appeared "dry and wilted" next to the themes he borrowed from Tchaikovsky.

Asafiev's book ends on a note of caution. He trusts Stravinsky's

[15] *Ibid.,* p. 99.

[16] *Ibid.,* p. 32.

[17] *Ibid.,* p. 7.

[18] On this point, Prokofiev disagrees with his friend Asafiev, to whom he writes, "Stravinsky's Piano Concerto continues the . . . stylization of Bach. I disapprove of this . . . Unfortunately, he thinks otherwise . . . He even believes that he is creating a new era . . ." I. Nestiev, *Prokofiev,* transl. F. Jonas, Stanford, 1960, p. 203. See also Prokofiev's *Autobiography,* p. 61.

[19] Asafiev, *Kniga . . .,* p. 364.

[20] *Ibid.,* p. 365. The "supra-national" aspect is ridiculed by Prokofiev in a letter to Miaskovsky (1927): "The librettist is French, the text Latin, the subject Greek, the music Anglo-German (after Handel), the performance will be in Monaco paid for by American money — indeed the height of Internationalism."

[21] *Ibid.,* pp. 386, 389.

"unerring instinct, sensitivity, and presentiment of historic necessity"[22] but he fears for his future. The Parisian "snobs" may desert him, and he may find himself without a public. Already his last ballets, notwithstanding their high intellectual standards, were disconcerting in their rootlessness. "The fate of Stravinsky's music will ultimately be decided, not in the West, but in the homeland that brought him up . . ."[23]

After Asafiev's death in 1949, the Moscow Academy of Science, honoring the memory of its distinguished member, sponsored a five-volume edition of his Collected Works. The *Book on Stravinsky* was not included. In his preface to the first volume, the composer Dmitri Kabalevsky refers to it as a "deeply erroneous apologia" written during Asafiev's period of "uncritical enthusiasm" for modern Western music, and continues, "In later years, Asafiev sharply condemned his own *Book on Stravinsky* and contrasted it with totally different, sober, and well-founded conclusions on the cosmopolitan and formalistic music of Stravinsky."[24]

It is true that during the musico-political crisis of 1948, Asafiev released a statement containing the following passage: "In the past, I wrote much on Stravinsky and I must admit that I, and many others, recognized in his work certain elements as progressive that, in fact, were only individualistic seditions. Like many petit-bourgeois insurgents, Stravinsky ended in the camp of blackest reaction."[25]

Too ill to deliver his report in person, Asafiev had it read to the First All-Union Congress of Soviet Composers. At least one Western observer, the British journalist Alexander Werth, expressed certain doubts: "The whole tone of the address was . . . so much in contradiction with what Asafiev had written only a few months before . . . that one can only conclude that it was very heavily subedited."[26]

A few other Russian publications on Stravinsky that appeared in the 1920s deserve brief mention. Two years before Asafiev's book was published, one of his close associates, Y. Vainkop, wrote a lengthy essay on Stravinsky which appeared as a booklet in a series devoted to contemporary composers.[27] In format and price, these brochures

[22] *Ibid.*, p. 396.

[23] *Ibid.*, p. 2. Further translated excerpts from Asafiev's book can be found in A. Olkhovsky, *Music under the Soviets*, New York, 1955, pp. 27-33.

[24] B. Asafiev, *Izbrannye Trudy* I, Moscow, 1952, p. 15.

[25] *Ibid.*, p. 15 f.

[26] A. Werth, *Musical Uproar in Moscow*, London, 1949, p. 97.

[27] Y. Vainkop, *Stravinsky*, Leningrad, 1927.

were aimed at wide popular distribution and reflected the strong interest in modern music prevalent among Russian audiences of the 1920s. Vainkop's essay presents a good deal of factual information as well as brief analyses of works. His approach is non-technical without being in the least condescending. He deals with Stravinsky as an admirer rather than a critic and calls him "the teacher of his era" who "began where others left off."

A booklet on *Les Noces* by Victor Belayev[28] calls it "a work of profound national importance." Like Asafiev, Belayev contrasts the "Mighty Five" with their "tendency to elaborate the Russian folk-melos" to Stravinsky's "return to the primitive, i.e. to genuine folk-melos." Far from having become "Europeanized," *Les Noces* confirms that Stravinsky "must be regarded as one of the most Russian composers who have ever existed." The question of Stravinsky's inner ties with his homeland was obviously uppermost in the minds of Soviet critics of the 1920s and is reflected in the impassioned Russianism of Belayev's (as well as Asafiev's) comments.

Another young disciple of Asafiev, Mikhail Druskin, dealt with a special aspect of Stravinsky's music — his novel piano style. In a book, *New Piano Music,*[29] he devotes several pages to a perceptive discussion of Stravinsky's keyboard works, from the early Etudes, Op. 7 (1908), to the Concerto, the Sonata, and the Serenade (1925). He is particularly fascinated by the *Piano Rag Music* (1919), which he calls the "turning point in contemporary piano literature" and "the gospel of modern rhythm." A few years later, in 1935, Druskin wrote a booklet on *Petrushka,*[30] displaying a more reserved approach which reflected the changing trend in Soviet musical thought. He defended Stravinsky against the reproach that his creative path followed the "zigzag of bourgeois artistic fashions" but had to admit that the composer was passing through an "ideological crisis." In calling Stravinsky "the most eminent master of contemporary music of the bourgeois West," Druskin stressed the composer's separation from his homeland.

*   *

*

[28] Victor M. Belayev, *I. Stravinsky's Les Noces,* transl. S. W. Pring, London, 1928. The date of the Russian edition (if any) cannot be ascertained. The author is not connected with the "Belayev circle," named after the publisher Mitrofan Belayev.

[29] M. Druskin, *Novaya Fortepiannaya Muzyka,* Leningrad, 1928.

[30] Y. Slonimsky and M. Druskin, *Petrushka,* Leningrad, 1935.

Early in the 1930s, the Association for Contemporary Music went out of existence. For a brief time, the radical Russian Association of Proletarian Musicians (RAPM) acquired a leading role until, in April 1932, a party decree dissolved all cultural proletarian groups. In the field of music, a single professional organization was established, the Union of Soviet Composers, with its own journal, *Sovietskaya Muzyka,* which began to appear in 1933. A new esthetic concept emerged — Socialist Realism —, extolled by Maxim Gorky at the First Conference of Soviet Writers in 1934 and soon extended to music. All Western-style modernistic trends were branded as "Formalism." Prokofiev, who had returned to Russia in 1933 after fifteen years abroad, quipped, "Formalism is sometimes the name given here to music not understood at first hearing." But the Soviet cultural arbiters proved their determination by publicly castigating Shostakovich in 1936.

In this tense atmosphere, a reappraisal of Stravinsky and of his relationship to Russian music was unavoidable. In 1933, a noted Soviet musicologist, Arnold Alshvang, published an essay, *The Ideological Path of Igor Stravinsky,*[31] which destroyed the aura of near-infallibility created by Asafiev and his school. In identifying Stravinsky with the hated prerevolutionary bourgeois class, he introduced a socio-political element into his musical criticism and established an effective pattern followed until today. His opening paragraph sets the tone:

Stravinsky is an important and near-comprehensive artistic ideologist of the imperialist bourgeoisie. With startling receptivity he has captured all the trends, all the changes in the psychology of his class; and together with his class, in these last years, he is moving swiftly towards his doom. This doom is exemplified by the colossal narrowing and the extreme impoverishment . . . of his great talent . . .

Young Stravinsky is described as a "national-Russian artist, with thoroughly Russian topicality, quaintly combined with elements of symbolism and European decadence." He was socially conditioned "by an artistic environment centered ideologically not in Russia, but in Paris." In Diaghilev's ballets, in Stravinsky's music, the Russian imperialist bourgeoisie joined the art of world bourgeoisie, became "Europeanized." Despite the outward brilliance, it is essentially a reactionary art, expressing itself in bourgeois stylizations of Russian peasant elements and formalistic idealizations of the distant past, done on the high technical level of the latest European urbanistic art.

[31] In *Sovietskaya Muzyka,* 1933, No. 5. The entire essay (except the opening paragraph) is reprinted in A. Alshvang, *Izbrannye Statii,* Moscow, 1959.

Alshvang does not question the significance of *Firebird, Petrushka, Sacre*: they are "the most brilliant products of musical Impressionism on Russian soil." Yet they are based on a "miniature" concept in which musical development is replaced by external contrasts. Stravinsky's further evolution reflected the general trend of bourgeois art — the negation of Impressionism. He moved from complexity to simplicity without abandoning piquant innovations. He created a sort of "musical Cubism" — amusing techniques of distortions and displacements, a negation of reality not based on humor but on "joyless mockery." The larger works of Stravinsky's "second" period (as Alshvang terms the years 1914-23), such as *L'Histoire du soldat, Pulcinella, Mavra, Les Noces,* are striking in their unusual instrumental combinations, mastery of varied genres, absorption of musico-historical material. But behind the brilliant exterior there is a decline and impoverishment of creative ideas, of musical values; they are filled with the pessimism so characteristic of post-war European art. Alshvang also criticizes the "Russian *émigré* topicality expressing itself in exaggerated representation of the Russian past, idealized in its most inert aspects." In fact, he finds that Stravinsky's "Russian" works, as a whole, do not reflect any outstanding traits of Russian reality; on the contrary, all stagnant and primordial customs are painted affectionately as if they represented "eternal" values.

After 1923, a new stylistic phase opened. Having absorbed jazz and exhausted the "émigré" topicality, Stravinsky sensed the changing artistic fashion in Paris and became the leading exponent of "Purism" — an "elevated" art free of all mockery and grotesqueness, detached from worldly existence. While his apologists try to explain the "philosophical" background of his newest works, the public is bored. Alshvang doubts Stravinsky's ability to achieve "sustained content" and finds some of his rivals (e.g. Hindemith, Honegger) richer despite the "deeply decadent content all bourgeois composers share." *Oedipus Rex* appears "deadly static" compared to Honegger's *Antigone,* while *L'Histoire* never achieves the "touching simplicity" of Kodály's *Háry János.*

Stravinsky's instrumental works written between 1923 and 1931 also strive towards an "elevated" style by using forms and devices of the past. Alshvang's criticism is devastating: "anemic, decadent thematic material . . . artificial cheerfulness with an occasional tear . . . inflections of the 'bookish' language of the 18th century . . . fallacious emphasis on constructivism . . . but above all the insufferable dryness, the extinction of emotional, lifelike function of a given musical genre under the disguise of an 'elevated' abstract language."[32] Even the few attractive pages (in the Piano Concerto, in *Oedipus*) sound like "noble" reminiscences of epigonal Romanticism. In the finale of the Capriccio Alshvang detects "pleasant echoes" of ballet music by Drigo and Delibes — "touching omniverousness," as he remarks sarcastically. The essay closes with an often paraphrased indictment: "Stravinsky is speeding irrevocably towards the void of unreality. Against this there is no recourse in the dense eclectic mixture of Handel, jazz, Tchaikovsky, the Catholic Mass, and Drigo!"[33]

Alshvang's essay, considered a major contribution to Soviet comment on Stravinsky and listed in all bibliographies, reflected the growing disenchantment of the Russian intelligentsia with Stravinsky's creative evolution. By 1933 it had become evident that his outer and inner ties with his Russian homeland were severed forever. Even his past "Russianism" became suspect, and a reappraisal of his Russian works from *Sacre* to *Mavra* and *Les Noces* made them appear as mockery and distortion of Russian historical reality. The injection of ideological criteria was to become ever more pronounced. In the case of Stravinsky, the latent antagonism was aggravated by the publication of his *Autobiography*[34] in 1935 and the *Poetics of Music*[35] (1939-40), which contained many views opposed to Soviet concepts.

*   *

*

The outbreak of the Second World War halted all esthetic controversies in the Soviet world of the arts. After the war, there was a vigorous revival of ideological vigilance which led to public condemnation of "formalist" aspects in literature, philosophy, and music. Following a conference between A. Zhdanov, ranking member of the Politbureau, and the Composers' Union, a decree was issued in February 1948, castigating the leading Soviet composers — Shostakovich, Prokofiev, Miaskovsky, Khachaturian, and others — for "disregarding the great social role of music."[36]

---

[32] Alshvang, *Izbrannye Statii,* p. 302.

[33] *Ibid.,* p. 303.

[34] *Chronique de ma vie,* Paris, 1935. English transl., New York, 1936, 1958.

[35] Charles Eliot Norton Lectures delivered at Harvard in 1939-40. Published in New York, 1942 (also in Paris as *Poétique musicale*).

[36] See N. Slonimsky, *Music Since 1900,* 3rd ed., New York, 1949, p. 684 f. Also A. Werth, *op. cit.*

The name of Stravinsky as the "apostle of reactionary forces in bourgeois music" was injected by the composer Tikhon Khrennikov, secretary of the Composers' Union. He traced formalistic ideas in Russian music to the reactionary period after the 1905 Revolution. Stravinsky's *Sacre* and Prokofiev's *Chout* are named as examples of "decadent" music. Their goal is escape from human reality into abstraction, according to Stravinsky's own words.[37] The *Sacre* expresses moods of "savagery and bestial instincts" through "boisterous, chaotic, intentionally coarse, screaming sonorities." In *Petrushka* and *Les Noces,* elements of Russian life are used to ridicule Russian customs and to emphasize "Russian Asianism, crudity, animal instincts, sexual motives." From Stravinsky's opera *Mavra* with its "grotesque distortions" there is a direct line to such "defective" works as *The Nose* and *Lady Macbeth* by Shostakovich. As to Stravinsky's "back to Bach" movement, it led to the *Symphony of Psalms,* "in which there are stridently combined the old Bachian devices of polyphonic writing with the ear-splitting 'contemporary' harmonies."[38]

Khrennikov's influential position made his declaration tantamount to an official policy statement. The chorus of invectives increased during the last years of Stalin's regime. The height of virulence was reached in an article, *Dollar Cacophony,* published in the newspaper *Izvestia* in 1951, dealing with the "wretchedness" of music in America from the Metropolitan Opera to Tin Pan Alley:

Capitalism is the enemy of culture . . . The United States is the most anti-musical country in the world . . . The shameless prophet of bourgeois modernists, Igor Stravinsky, having found a haven in the U.S.A., says outright: "The broad masses contribute nothing to art. They cannot raise its level." In another article he admits even more openly: "My music today does not express anything that can be suspected of reality." Indeed, the works of this rootless cosmopolitan testify to the complete inner impoverishment . . . [39]

The antagonism towards the West went hand in hand with an effort to eradicate all traces of Western influence on Russian music, past and present. A curious by-product was the elimination of foreign references in bibliographies. On comparing the "Stravinsky" articles in two different editions of the *Great Soviet Encyclopedia,* one finds that the earlier edition (1947) lists foreign as well as Russian source

[37] Stravinsky, *What I Wished to Express in the* Sacre, in *Muzyka,* 1913, No. 141.

[38] Slonimsky, *op. cit.,* pp. 694-96. Original text in *Sovietskaya Muzyka,* 1948, No. 1.

[39] *Izvestia,* Jan. 7, 1951. The article is signed by I. Nestiev.

materials while the "second edition" (1956) limits the bibliography to Russian-language sources. Significantly, both editions fail to mention Asafiev's *Book on Stravinsky* as well as any of the laudatory studies published in the 1920s.

*   *

*

The period following Stalin's death in 1953 is often referred to as "The Thaw." In musical circles the atmosphere became generally more relaxed, discussions were encouraged, cultural contacts with the West were reestablished, foreign musicians and scholars were once again welcomed. The culmination came in 1958, when a new party decree reversed some of the injustices of the 1948 decree, blaming them on "J. V. Stalin's subjective approach to certain works of art."[40] While the new decree vindicated Shostakovich and (posthumously) Prokofiev and Miaskovsky, it firmly upheld the esthetic principle of Socialist Realism.

In view of this *détente,* it is surprising to find that Soviet evaluation of Stravinsky has remained virtually unchanged during the past ten years. There is continuing antagonism, directed as much against his ideas as against his music. His thoughts on music and musicians, as expressed in the *35 Questions and Answers* (1957),[41] touched off a bitter controversy: his endorsement of Webern and dodecaphonism was derided, his slurs on Russian and Soviet music were resented. His later works — *The Rake's Progress, Canticum sacrum, Agon, Threni* — were subjected to scathing criticism. Addressing a Moscow audience in 1959, Leonard Bernstein exclaimed, "There are two Stravinskys and I love them both!" "Impossible," replied a Soviet critic, "the traits of decay and creativity in music are incompatible."[42] Annoyed by Bernstein's remark that the *Sacre* had not been heard in Russia in over thirty years,[43] the critic spoke of Stravinsky's "tragic period . . . when the composer (in emigration, separated from his Russian national roots)

[40] The decree (dated May 28) was published in *Pravda* on June 8, 1958, with detailed commentary. English translation in *Current Digest* X:23 (July 16, 1958).

[41] Published originally in the British magazine *Encounter,* although Soviet critics usually quote from a German translation which appeared in *Melos* (June 1957; Feb. 1958). Incorporated into the *Conversations* by Stravinsky and Craft, New York, 1958.

[42] *Sovietskaya Kultura,* Aug. 27, 1959.

[43] The allegation was refuted: *Sacre* was performed in Tallinn "as recently as last year," also fragments were staged in Leningrad and Kiev (Moscow was not mentioned).

took the road of open cosmopolitanism." This led him to the "dodeca-phonic Cantata St. Mark, the graveyard of decomposed musical com-position . . . the work in which Stravinsky destroyed himself."[44]

This work, the *Canticum sacrum,* was the subject of a more thorough, but no less devastating, essay entitled *Holy Cacophony* by I. Nestiev.[45] It opens with a calculated slur — a motto drawn from Gogol's *A Madman's Diary* (1835), where the protagonist muses over a dog's letter: "Strangely uneven style. One can see immediately that it was not written by a human. It starts the way it should be, and ends in a dog-like manner."

Nestiev's introductory remarks deal with Stravinsky's "creative 'uni-versality' ": "He can make any kind of music, in any style and for any purpose: Catholic Mass, circus polka, modernized jazz, ballets on most eccentric themes . . ." Now comes his surprising "conversion" to "fashionable dodecaphony, which he had criticized severely for many years."

Nestiev reviews the *Canticum* on the basis of a piano score. The music repels him by its "cold speculativeness" and a strange combina-tion of "tedious calculation and unbridled anarchy of sound." The reviewer distinguishes two elements: the stark ascetic Gothic world of the 14th century (modernized through intentionally harsh and willful combinations of sound), and the no less scholastic but "far more re-volting dodecaphonic 'music' where natural inflections are replaced by ugly and labored 'geometry of sound'." He continues:

Both these seemingly contrasting elements appear related in Stravinsky's treat-ment: they carefully avoid any living melodic thought conceived by a human heart and capable of evoking a warm response in the soul of a normal listener. In the *Canticum* there is literally not a single natural inflection. It is a dead desert, barren and stony . . . How ravaged, how emasculated must have been the soul of the composer capable of creating such dreadful music . . .[46]

This review (which goes into considerable detail) is a fairly charac-teristic example of Soviet reaction to Stravinsky's "dodecaphonic" style. There is a monolithic implacability in the Soviet rejection that is beyond all discussion. The intellectual processes underlying twelve-tone tech-nique have been anathema to Soviet theorists for some three decades.

[44] *Sovietskaya Kultura,* Aug. 27, 1959.
[45] *Sovietskaya Muzyka,* 1958, No. 2, pp. 132-35.
[46] *Ibid.,* p. 132 f.

When Stravinsky embraced Webern, old and new antipathies were compounded to form an insuperable barrier.

These problems were explored soberly by Yuri Keldysh in an article, *The Ballet* Agon *and the "New Period" of Igor Stravinsky*.[47] He uses the analysis by Lawrence Morton which appeared after the première of *Agon*,[48] complete with tone row and musical examples, without disputing its main points. In fact, Keldysh concedes Stravinsky's "inventiveness in combining various instruments, searching for unusually tense tonal effects, sometimes merely puzzling to the listener, sometimes however not lacking a certain purely phonic charm."

This factual account is followed by an attempt to answer the question, "What is the significance of Stravinsky's 'dodecaphonic period,' and is it connected with a fundamental reappraisal and change of his previous esthetic principles?" While Keldysh admits that Stravinsky's latest works differ from those composed in the 1930s and 1940s, he feels that the composer preserved his characteristic "handwriting" and did not change into a commonplace epigone of Webern. "Stravinsky does not sacrifice the old in favor of the new, but assimilates the procedures of serial technique, adapting them to the established norms of musical thought known to him."

Keldysh's subsequent discussion of Stravinsky's "adaptability" offers nothing new: he accuses him of remaining coldly indifferent to inner content regardless of what "disguise" he wears. Western quotations are used to bolster this contention (Olivier Messiaen's saying "the man of 1001 styles"). For Stravinsky, composing is a "game with given rules"[49] or "a way of fashioning works according to certain methods acquired either by apprenticeship or by inventiveness."[50] This leads Keldysh to conclude that the "artistic material" is a matter of indifference to Stravinsky — the main thing is the "method," the "game." Hence he is able to switch easily from one style to another, to write parodies of other eras and other composers, and to accomplish without effort his latest "vault" to dodecaphony. He merely acquired a new mask, like the many-faced deity who, behind all disguises, always remains the same. Keldysh contends that Stravinsky's latest shift (like all previous ones) was not dictated by "inner organic necessity" but simply by fear

[47] *Sovietskaya Muzyka*, 1960, No. 8, pp. 166-79.
[48] *The Musical Quarterly*, October 1957, pp. 535-41.
[49] A. Tansman, *Igor Stravinsky*, New York, 1949, p. 9.
[50] Stravinsky, *Poetics of Music*, reprint New York, 1956, p. 24 f.

lest he "lag behind his time," and supports his contention with quotations from the Stravinsky-Craft *Conversations*.

Nevertheless, Stravinsky's endorsement of dodecaphony is not to be taken as a "casual episode": it is symptomatic of the search for a "common denominator" in modernistic art.[51] Actually, "reactionary bourgeois art" dangles helplessly between "sober rationalism and ecstatic mysticism," all caused by the "mortal loneliness of the artist in a capitalist society." The two extremes are represented by Stravinsky and Schoenberg. In fact, the "high-strung Expressionism" of Schoenberg made him unacceptable to Stravinsky, to whom music is "an element of speculation" governed by some metaphysical "order." Both, however, "deny functional harmony." Keldysh warns against considering Stravinsky a champion of "tonal thinking" and explains his rejection of the term "atonality" in favor of "anti-tonality." All of Stravinsky's abstract "order" is nothing but pure licence governed superficially by rule and logic, Keldysh concludes; once some unifying, organizational principle was found in atonal music, Stravinsky felt free to accept the system. Thus, "the dodecaphonic phase of Stravinsky testifies . . . to further creative deterioration, sad senile debility, and complete barrenness of imagination, all carefully concealed behind false protestations extolling Webern's dogma which receives a somewhat belated recognition on the part of Stravinsky."

Keldysh ends his essay with a brief survey of Stravinsky's historical role in the development of modern ballet. Objections to his ballet style were raised as early as 1913 in connection with the *Sacre*. During the last years of his life, Diaghilev was allegedly cooling towards Stravinsky, whose *Baiser de la fée* (1928) he called "stillborn." The dancer and choreographer Serge Lifar is quoted as saying, "Stravinsky's music does not excite to dance; on the contrary, it kills it."[52] Keldysh finds "much truth" in Lifar's outburst and concludes that Stravinsky's path in the ballet led "not to rejuvenation, but to a deep crisis of the genre and to an undermining of its fundamentals." His music "robbed the dance of poetic animation . . . coarsened and subjugated it to motoric rhythm." As for *Agon,* "the score cannot be translated fully into the language of the dance." He finds that "the extreme rhythmic complexity, artificiality of design, and complete lack of esthetic breathing

[51] Here Keldysh refers to K. H. Fuessl, *Selbstbesinnung am Beispiel Stravinskys,* in *Oesterreichische Musikzeitung,* 1958, No. 11.

[52] S. Lifar, *I. Stravinsky législateur de ballet,* in *Revue musicale,* May-June 1939.

not only fail to invite dance, but actually inhibit the plasticity of movement." That Stravinsky has for years been able to dictate his will unto
the ballet theater only bespeaks the "complete esthetic chaos and confusion of all criteria" in contemporary modernistic art.

*   *

*

Such reviews, written by noted authorities,[53] carry particular weight
in the Soviet Union; for the reader is unable to compare the critic's
judgment with his own since the works under discussion are not performed in his country. The result is a preconceived negative opinion
without the countercheck of an actual listening experience.

This becomes abundantly clear when one reads the chapters on
Stravinsky in recent Soviet Russian textbooks. The *History of Russian
Music* by Keldysh devotes a substantial chapter of twenty pages to
"Igor Stravinsky and Musical Modernism."[54] The three-volume history
is used as a textbook in conservatories. The opening sentence of the
chapter in question sets the tone: "Stravinsky's creative work is the
most accomplished expression of the reactionary essence of modernism
as an anti-folk trend in art, reflecting the decadent ideology of the
imperialist bourgeoisie." Here, as in Alshvang's essay twenty years
earlier, we find the injection of ideological criteria that we have come
to expect in Soviet criticism. But Keldysh goes farther: he arrives at a
total rejection of Stravinsky and his works on musical, esthetic, and
ideological grounds. While previous Soviet views conceded certain
positive values to *Firebird* and *Petrushka,* Keldysh condemns even those
works because they allegedly distort and cheapen Russian folk material.
The *Sacre* is represented as the "crystalization" of the composer's "formalistic" tendencies. Later "Russian" works, such as *Pribaoutki, Renard,
Les Noces,* are termed "crude distortions" because folkloristic materials
are used for "willful experiments." In the opera *Mavra,* Russian inflections of the 19th century are "grotesquely caricatured." An uniden-
tified quotation from Asafiev describes Stravinsky as the "hammerer
of Russian melody." Although *L'Histoire* is based on a Russian tale,
Stravinsky chose to give it a "timeless" element permitting him to juxta-
pose the most heterogeneous styles and genres without an inner mo-
tivation.

[53] See also D. Kabalevsky's negative review of *The Rake's Progress* in *Sovietskaya Muzyka,* 1953, No. 10, pp. 72-73.
[54] Yuri Keldysh, *Istoria Russkoi Muzyki,* Moscow, Vols. 1 & 2, 1948; Vol. 3,
1954. Stravinsky chapter in Vol. 3, pp. 481-501.

Having devoted more than seventeen pages to the "Russian" works (including ten musical examples drawn from *Firebird, Petrushka, Sacre,* and *Les Noces*), Keldȳsh limits the remaining works to a discussion barely two pages long. After the break with his homeland, Stravinsky became a "citizen of the world" yet remained a stranger everywhere. He exploited "parasitically" the materials of various times and peoples, from ancient Greece to modern America ("with its cult of the dollar and jazz"). As evidences of the alleged "borrowings" by Stravinsky are enumerated the *Symphony of Psalms, Apollon Musagète, Pulcinella,* and *Baiser de la fée,* each with a subtly denigrating sentence. Mentioned are also the "neo-Classical stylizations 'à la Bach' with a sharp seasoning of cacophonic jazz sounds." The final paragraph is a bitter indictment:

Stravinsky's path is one of continuous decline and degradation . . . In our days, he is in fact a creatively dead figure. His latest works . . . represent a glaring example of complete degeneration, disregard for law, and coarseness of contemporary fascistized imperialist "culture" . . . The utterly formalist, decadent music of Stravinsky is deeply alien and inimical to the spirit of the high ideological art of our country. [55]

In mentioning Stravinsky's "latest works," Keldysh leaves his reader guessing, for nowhere in his text does he refer to any composition later than the *Symphony of Psalms* of 1930. In a volume designed as a textbook for young professionals, this one-sided stress on Stravinsky's "pseudo-Russian" aspects at the expense of some twenty-five years of later development is particularly incomprehensible.

Yet, exactly the same "arrangement" prevails in the newest *History of Russian Music,*[56] published as a conservatory textbook in 1959-60. Here, too, we find the overemphasis on the early works: out of a total of five pages, more than four are given to a discussion of *Firebird, Petrushka,* and *Sacre.* The further development of Stravinsky is dealt with in fifteen lines, and the most recent work mentioned is *Jeu de cartes* (1936). No attempt is made to discuss his instrumental works of the "neo-Classical" 1920s nor is there any mention of his latest evolution towards dodecaphony. The author of the Stravinsky chapter is L. Danilevich, a critic and former editor of *Sovietskaya Muzyka.* His contribution is a rather impersonal distillation of prevailing views, perhaps somewhat milder in tone than the Keldysh essay. It is also far shorter (five pages as compared to twenty) and uses only three musical examples, all drawn from *Petrushka,* mainly to illustrate Stravinsky's "daring"

[55] *Ibid.,* p. 501.
[56] *Istoria Russkoi Muzyki* (see note 1), III, 318-23.

and his "wrong harmonizations" of Russian folk tunes. "Without doubt, Stravinsky portrays, not the people in the true sense of the word, but a drunken mob. Connected with it is the grotesque, caricaturized treatment of folk material."[57] But at least the *Firebird* is restored to favor; its music bespeaks the "talent of the author and his orchestral mastery." In the *Sacre,* however, "the unwieldy harmonic combinations and cunning interlacings of rhythms and timbres" are criticized. In summarizing Stravinsky's further development, Danilevich falls back on well-worn generalities about the replacement of "living thought and human feelings with formalist abstractions, 'musical geometry,' . . . a constructivism consisting of . . . grotesquery, cold irony, skepticism, derision of life." No specific works are mentioned to support these contentions. There is a subtle effort to play down Stravinsky's significance for our time: "At one time the bourgeois critics were considerably surprised by the zigzags of Stravinsky's creative path in whose music there is a whimsical combination of jazz and Catholic chant, restoration of Lully and contemporary urbanism."[58] This last sentence reads like a paraphrase of the final statement in Alshvang's essay, almost thirty years back.

One of the latest and most comprehensive evaluations of Stravinsky is contained in a book on contemporary music by the noted musicologist, Grigory Shneyerson, entitled *On Music, Alive and Dead.*[59] Here a critique of Stravinsky's music is interspersed with extensive quotations from his writings. The passages selected are controversial from the Soviet point of view and give the author an opportunity to polemicize against Stravinsky's opinions.

Like most Soviet critics, Shneyerson paints a highly unsympathetic picture of Stravinsky's personality. In seeking an explanation for Stravinsky's "chameleonic" behavior, the Western critics lack the courage to say outright that "the esthetic instability of Stravinsky is the direct outgrowth of his reactionary ideology, his moral waste, his unbelief in the ethical power of his art."[60]

In discussing Stravinsky's music, Shneyerson is more conciliatory. The *Firebird* and *Petrushka* are restored to the rank of masterpieces; even the *Sacre* achieves qualified acceptance despite the "strange mixture of folkish elements with crude, offensive . . . conglomerations."

[57] *Ibid.,* p. 321.
[58] *Ibid.,* p. 323.
[59] Grigory Shneyerson, *O Muzyke zhyvoi i mertvoi,* Moscow, 1960, pp. 138-58.
[60] *Ibid.,* p. 145.

After Stravinsky's break with Russian tradition, "which in many ways conditioned the sensational novelty and originality of his earlier works," the seach for allegedly "new" paths led him to the reactionary esthetics of neo-Classicism. Yet, in this period — side by side with much "stale constructivism"—he also produced a few "very interesting and sparkling scores." Mentioned are the "colorful stylizations" of *Baiser de la fée* (previously termed a "potpourri-like conglomeration") and *Pulcinella* (called "decadent" not long ago), also *Les Noces* with a "fresh harmonic and polyphonic texture" and "original instrumentation" (only recently described as "the height of constructivist absurdity and unnaturalness"). These are attempts at reappraisal, modest yet significant.

Shneyerson is the first Soviet author to attempt an (admittedly superficial) assessment of Stravinsky's "American" period. He finds it characteristic that the American atmosphere, the necessity of adjusting to a new manner of life and to "totally different demands of the audiences," forced Stravinsky to reorient himself quickly. In order to strengthen his position in the U.S.A. and to win favor with the broad public, Stravinsky extends the scope of his work "from jazz to Mass, from symphony to circus polka." Without entirely abandoning his neo-Classic style, the composer adapts himself easily to the most variegated demands. Enumerated are such heterogeneous works and commissions as the *Scherzo à la russe* for Paul Whiteman, the *Ebony Concerto* for Woody Herman, the *Dumbarton Oaks Concerto* for the "millionaire Robert Bliss." The Mass is mentioned as signifying Stravinsky's conversion to the Roman Catholic faith — a rumor so persistent that Stravinsky found it necessary to deny it recently.[61] In listing the symphonies, Shneyerson quotes with irony the various dedications: the "bloodless" *Symphony of Psalms* "written to the glory of God and dedicated to the Boston Orchestra"; the Symphony in C "dedicated to God Almighty and the Chicago Orchestra"; and the Symphony in Three Movements "dedicated to the New York Philharmonic (this time without reference to the Almighty)." Even the *Star-Spangled Banner* is drawn into this list of "failures": Stravinsky's orchestration caused a near-riot in Boston, where the public was indignant because of his "licence and distortion."

Stravinsky's shift to the "dodecaphonic faith" is dramatized as a "new sharp break":

A man, bereft of his homeland . . . must now, in his declining years, in order to maintain the public interest in his fading music, engage in doubtful dode-

[61] *Expositions and Developments,* p. 65.

caphonic experiments about which he spoke contemptuously all his life . . . It is difficult to believe in the sincerity of an artist who so easily switches his creative aims . . . from one extreme to the other, denying today what only yesterday was the essence of his artistic creed . . .[62]

Forgetting his own principle, "never to follow a system," Stravinsky chose as his model Anton Webern's complex system of "total" organization. Once again he confounded Western critics who search in vain for a "common denominator" that could be applied to the continually shifting image of Stravinsky. Shneyerson relates with obvious relish the utter confusion in the various critical camps ranging from the "apologists" of serialism to the opponents of dodecaphony.

As was to be expected, Stravinsky's latest scores — *Canticum sacrum, Agon, Threni* — are discussed as a hopeless cul-de-sac. Shneyerson points to the somewhat freer use of serial technique in *Agon,* possibly induced by the element of the dance, and illustrates this with thirteen measures from the *Pas de deux.* All the stricter is the score of *Threni,* which is called a "cold dodecaphonic construction." Even equipped with "dodecaphonic blinders," Stravinsky wants to be original: he insists that "serial" technique does not prevent him from being a "tonal" composer. This assertion (reinforced by a quotation from the *Conversations*) strikes Shneyerson as arbitrary and contradictory. Stravinsky's recent inclination towards Church-connected music (*Canticum, Threni*) is interpreted as a "panicky flight from contemporary reality," while his efforts to draft serial technique upon liturgical music are allegedly dictated by his fear of appearing an "outmoded academician." But "neither the Pope nor Webern is able to uphold the growing creative decrepitude of an artist who once gave to the world the wonders of *Firebird* and *Petrushka,* or to return to him his past belief in his art, in his muse, in himself . . ."[63]

In offering numerous translated excerpts from Stravinsky's writings, Shneyerson performs an important service for the many Soviet readers to whom the original texts are either incomprehensible or inaccessible. Certain pages are given without comment, for example the description of Stravinsky's early relationship with his teacher, Rimsky-Korsakov, taken from the *Autobiography.* Other excerpts, however, are selected for their controversial value, to prove Stravinsky's incorrigible "formalism." Taken out of context, many of the quotations must strike the Soviet reader as completely heretical.

[62] Shneyerson, *op. cit.,* p. 144 f.
[63] *Ibid.,* p. 158.

A good illustration is the sentence "Music is powerless to express anything at all," much quoted by East and West. Recently, Stravinsky felt compelled to comment on "that overpublicized bit about expression (or non-expression)," which he termed "offhand and annoyingly incomplete";[64] nevertheless he classified those who took it literally as "stupider critics." Another statement of Stravinsky gained wide notoriety in Soviet circles: "The mass, in relation to art, is a quantitative term which never once entered into my considerations . . . The broad mass adds nothing to the art, they cannot raise the level, and the artist who aims consciously at 'mass-appeal' can do so only by lowering his own level . . ."[65] That Stravinsky is inclined to be contemptuous of his audience was deduced from his *Autobiography* by Shneyerson and other Soviet writers. Much criticized is also Stravinsky's attitude towards folklore, which to him is mainly raw material. On this point, there is a fundamental difference of opinion between Asafiev, who considered Stravinsky's approach truly creative yet authentic,[66] and the later Soviet position castigating the alleged "distortions" of Russian heritage.

In the *Poetics of Music,* Stravinsky antagonized Soviet critics by his provocative views on music and the creative processes, which were termed "reactionary." Highly controversial from the Soviet viewpoint is the fifth chapter, "The Avatars of Russian Music." Nevertheless, Soviet writers appear familiar with Stravinsky's *apologia* (as he calls the *Poetics*) and make good use of its crisp, aphoristic formulations.

The scorn and indignation aroused by the *35 Questions and Answers*[67] had two entirely separate motivations. One reason could be dealt with coolly and ironically — Stravinsky's endorsement of Webern's serialism and his favorable comments on the ultra-modern schools of composition. The other reason, however, was emotional and created a commensurate reaction — Stravinsky's slurring remarks on certain aspects of Russian and Soviet music. (That similar ideas were already expressed in the *Poetics* was obviously overlooked).

Shortly after the *Questions and Answers* appeared in the West

---

[64] *Expositions and Developments,* p. 114 f.

[65] Quoted by Shneyerson, *op. cit.,* p. 152 f., after *Musical Digest,* Sept. 1956.

[66] In addition to the *Book on Stravinsky,* see also B. Asafiev, *Russian Music from the Beginning of the 19th Century,* Moscow, 1930; English transl. by A. J. Swan, Ann Arbor, Mich., 1953, pp. 43-44, 85-87, 191, 197. In *Les Noces,* Belayev (*op. cit.*) found the "genuineness . . . beyond dispute."

[67] See note 41.

German journal *Melos,* a detailed review (or rather rebuttal), which was both factual and emotional, was published in *Sovietskaya Muzyka.*[68] "History never forgives those who renounce the homeland — whether they be politicians, artists, or writers . . ." As for Stravinsky's endorsement of serialism, it is dismissed as the "last refuge of one who has betrayed the high ideals of a humanistic art and has found himself irretrievably in the morass of cosmopolitanism."

Shneyerson takes a similar, though more dispassionate, attitude, at least towards the technical aspects of dodecaphonism. He devotes several pages to quoting Stravinsky's thoughts on the creative process, on harmony, on serial technique, on Webern's significance. He cannot suppress the remark that Stravinsky's "genuflection" before the muse of Webern is "laughable" in view of his life-long opposition to twelve-tone technique. But Shneyerson becomes emotional, too, when he castigates Stravinsky for "offending the memory of Tchaikovsky and the Mighty Five" and for "turning his back on Soviet music" while praising the "delirious works of German and French pointillists and concretniki."

*   *

*

The polemics aroused by Stravinsky's writings underline the dual problem faced by Soviet criticism — his music and his ideology. To the Soviet mind, they appear inextricably intertwined; for most of Stravinsky's written comments concern the essence of music — *his* music as well as the art and science of music in its broader aspects. These comments and ideas are, for the most part, diametrically opposed to Soviet concepts. "In his literary works, Stravinsky must be regarded as an ideologist of formalism and cosmopolitanism," declares the *Great Soviet Encyclopedia* with finality.[69] Thus, for the Soviet critic, the problem is whether to evaluate the totality of Stravinsky's personality or to admit a dichotomy between his ideas and his music.

There can be little doubt that, sooner or later, much of Stravinsky's music will be heard again in the Soviet Union. Some of the present barriers seem artificial: certainly, neo-Classicism is no more "reactionary" in the works of Stravinsky than in those by Prokofiev, Milhaud, Poulenc, which are accepted cheerfully. Nor is Stravinsky more "cacophonous" than, for example, Bartók, who is played in the Soviet Union.

[68] *Sovietskaya Muzyka,* 1957, No. 10, pp. 122-24.

[69] *Bolshaya Sovietskaya Encyclopedia,* 2nd ed., Moscow, 1956, Vol. 41, **article** *Stravinsky.*

There is a clamor for a broadening of the musical repertory in the USSR[70] which has led to the already mentioned performance of Stravinsky's *Symphonies for Winds.* A review of the all-Stravinsky ballet program at the New York City Center (*Ebony Concerto, Apollon Musagète, Agon, Monumentum Gesualdo*), written by Ivan Martynov for *Sovietskaya Muzyka,*[71] reveals a perfect enjoyment of the music. Khrennikov's personal visit to Stravinsky's home in California and the invitation to come to the Soviet Union is an indication that old grudges may soon be laid to rest.[72] One fact is undeniable and may some day be recognized with pride: for the first time in the history of music, Russia has given to the world a truly leading figure in contemporary music — Igor Fedorovich Stravinsky.

[70] *Sovietskaya Muzyka,* 1962, No. 2, p. 99.

[71] *Ibid.,* 1962, No. 1, pp. 128-29. Martynov and Keldysh were the two Soviet delegates to the Eighth Congress of the International Musicological Society in New York, 1961.

[72] Stravinsky states his view with unsentimental candor: "Nostalgia has no part in my proposed visit to Russia. My wish to go there is due primarily to the evidence I have received of a genuine desire or need for me by the younger generation of Russian musicians. No artist's name has been more abused in the Soviet Union than mine, but one cannot achieve the future we must achieve with the Russians by nursing a grudge." (*Newsweek,* May 21, 1962.)

A SELECTED BIBLIOGRAPHY OF IGOR STRAVINSKY

Compiled by CARROLL D. WADE

I. BOOKS AND ARTICLES BY STRAVINSKY
II. BOOKS ABOUT STRAVINSKY
III. PERIODICAL ARTICLES DEVOTED TO STRAVINSKY
IV. REFERENCES TO SPECIFIC WORKS IN PERIODICALS

Abbreviations

A   Der Auftakt. Prague.
AM   Atlantic Monthly. Boston.
AMz   Allgemeine Musikzeitung. Berlin.
Ar   Arts. Paris.
BdS   Blätter der Staatsoper. Berlin.
C   Counterpoint. San Francisco.
Ch   The Chesterian. London.
CM   Cahiers musicaux. Brussels.
Co   Contrepoints. Paris.
CO   Current Opinion.
D   The Dominant. London.
DI   Dance Index. New York.
DM   Dansk Musiktidsskrift. Copenhagen.
DT   Dancing Times. London.
E   Etude. Philadelphia.
ER   The English Review.
HF   High Fidelity. New York.
HMR   Harvard Musical Review. Cambridge, Mass.
IM   International Musician. St. Louis.
JMT   Journal of Music Theory. New Haven, Conn.
JR   Juilliard Review. New York.
M   Melos. Mainz.
MA   Musical America. New York.

Ma   Musica. Paris.
MC   Musical Courier. New York.
MdA   Anbruch. Vienna.
MdZ   Musik der Zeit. Bonn.
MF   Musical Forecast. Pittsburgh.
MG   Musik und Gesellschaft. Wolfenbüttel.
Mia   Musicalia. Havana.
MK   Musik und Kirche. Kassel.
Mk   Die Musik. Stuttgart.
Ml   Le Ménestrel. Paris.
M&L   Music and Letters. London.
MM   Modern Music. New York.
MMu   Le Monde musical. Paris.
MO   Música d'oggi. Milan.
MQ   The Musical Quarterly. New York.
Mq   Musique. Paris.
MR   Music Review. London.
MS   Music Survey.
MSt   Musical Standard. London.
MT   Musical Times. London.
Muz   De Muziek. Amsterdam.
N   Music Library Association Notes. Washington.
NA   Nation and Athenaeum
NMR   New Music Review. New York.

NMZ Neue Musik Zeitschrift.
       Munich.
NM-Z Neue Musik-Zeitung. Cologne.
Nos Nosotros. Mexico, D.F.
NR   New Republic. New York.
NRF Nouvelle revue française.
       Paris.
O   Opera. London.
OM   Oesterreichische Musikzeit-
       schrift. Vienna.
ON   Opera News. New York.
P   Il Pianoforte. Turin.
PR   Partisan Review. New York.
RaM Rassegna musicale. Turin.
RM   Revue musicale. Paris.

RMB Revue musicale belge. Brussels.
RP   Revue Pleyel. Paris.
S   The Score. London.
Sig Signale für die musikalische
       Welt. Leipzig.
SIM S.I.M. La Revue musicale.
       Paris.
SM   Schweitzerische Musikzeitung.
       Zurich.
SR   Saturday Review. New York.
S&S Science and Society.
St   Stimmen. Berlin.
T   Tempo. London.
TM   Les Temps modernes. Paris.
ZfM Zeitschrift für Musik. Mainz.

*   *

*

I. Books and Articles by Stravinsky

Stravinsky et Tchaikovsky. RM, III/9 (1922), 87-88.

Stravinsky Previsions a New Music. CO, LXXVIII (1925), 329-30.

Chronological Progress in Musical Art. E, XLIV/8 (1926), 559-60.

Avertissement . . . A Warning. D, I/2 (1927), 13-14.

Why People Dislike My Music. MF, XVII/6, (1930), 1, 12.

Avant le Sacre. RM, XVI/152 (1935), 1-14.

Chroniques de ma vie. Paris: Denoel et Stcele, 1935, 2 vols.

Chronicle of My Life. Transl. from the French. London: Gollancz, 1936, 286 pp.

Early Musical Influence in My Life. E, LV/3 (1936), 155-56.

Erinnerungen. Zürich-Berlin: Atlantis-Verlag, 1937, 227 pp.

Poétique musicale sous forme de six leçons. (Charles Eliot Norton Lectures for 1939-40.) Cambridge, Mass.: Harvard Univ. Press, 1942, 94 pp.

Poétique musicale. Dijon: J. B. Janin, 1945, 166 pp.

Ueber den Vortag. M, XIV (1946), 6-8.

Poetics of Music in the Form of Six Lessons. Transl. by Arthur Knodel and Ingolf Dahl. Cambridge, Mass.: Harvard Univ. Press, 1947, xi, 142 pp.

Musikalische Poetik. Übers. von Heinrich Strobel. Mainz: Schott's Söhne, 1949, 80 pp.

Poétique musicale. Nouv. éd. rev. et complétée. Paris: Éditions Le Bon Plaisir, 1952, 97 pp.

The Diaghilev I Knew. AM, CXCII (1953), 33-36.

Reflections on the Rake: the Origin of the Music. ON, XVII/15 (1953), 8.

Poetics of Music in the Form of Six Lessons. Transl. by Arthur Knodel and Ingolf Dahl. Preface by Darius Milhaud. New York: Vintage Books, 1956, viii, 146 pp.

Stravinsky on Schönberg, "Genius," Verdi, etc. [with Robert Craft]. SR, XL/45 (1957), 36-37.

Leben und Werk, von ihm selbst. Zürich: Atlantis-Verlag, 1957, 344 pp.

Mein Leben. Vollständige Ausgabe. Munich: P. List, 1958, 170 pp.

Apropos "Le Sacre du Printemps." SR, XLII/52 (1959), 29-31, 37.

Conversations with Igor Stravinsky. By I. Stravinsky and Robert Craft. Garden City, N. Y.: Doubleday, 1959, 162 pp.

Memories and Commentaries. By Igor Stravinsky and Robert Craft. Garden City, N. Y.: Doubleday, 1960, 167 pp.

"Firebird's" First Flight. HF, Oct. 1960, pp. 34-36.

Expositions and Developments. By Igor Stravinsky and Robert Craft. Garden City, N. Y.: Doubleday, 1962, 192 pp.

II. BOOKS ABOUT STRAVINSKY

Ackere, Jules van. *Igor Stravinsky.* Antwerp: Standaard-Boekhandel, 1954, 59 pp.

Adorno, Theodore W. *Philosophie der neuen Musik.* Tübingen: Mohr, 1949, vii, 144 pp.

Armitage, Merle [editor]. *Igor Strawinsky.* New York: G. Schirmer, 1936, 158 pp.

Avec Stravinsky: textes d'Igor Stravinsky et al. Lettres inédites de Claude Debussy [et al.] Monaco: Editions du Rocher, 1958, 215 pp.

Boulanger, Nadia. *Lectures on Modern Music* delivered under the auspices of the Rice Institute lectureship in Music, Jan. 27, 28, 29, 1925. Houston, Texas: The Rice Institute, 1926, pp. 113-95. (Includes *Stravinsky.*)

Casella, Alfredo. *Igor Strawinski.* Rome: A. F. Formíggini, 1926, 64 pp.

Casella, Alfredo. *Strawinski.* Nuova ed., con un capitolo di aggiornamento di Guglielmo Barblan. Brescia: La Scuola, 1951, 247 pp.

Cirlot, Juan Eduardo. *Igor Strawinsky; su tiempo, su significación, su obra.* Barcelona: Editorial G. Gili, 1949, 218 pp.

Collaer, Paul. *Strawinsky.* Brussels: Editions "Equilibres," 1930, 163 pp.

Corle, Edwin [editor]. *Igor Strawinsky.* New York: Duell, Sloan and Pearce, distributors, 1949, 249 pp.

Fleischer, Herbert. *Strawinsky.* Berlin, New York: Russischer Musik Verlag, 1931, 5, 286 pp.

Handschin, Jacques. *Igor Strawinski, Versuch einer Einführung.* Zürich, Leipzig: Kommissions-Verlag, Hug & Cie., 1933, 38 pp.

Igor Strawinsky [zum siebzigsten Geburtstag]. Mit Beiträgen von W. H. Auden [et al]. (Musik der Zeit; eine Schriftenreihe zur zeitgenössischen Musik). Bonn: Boosey & Hawkes, 1952, 78 pp.

Igor Strawinsky. A Complete Catalogue of his Published Works. London: Boosey & Hawkes, 1957.

Kirchmeyer, Helmut. *Igor Strawinsky:* Zeitgeschichte im Persönlichkeitsbild; Grundlagen und Voraussetzungen zur modernen Konstruktionstechnik. (Kölner Beiträge zur Musikforschung, 10.) Regensburg: G. Bosse, 1958, xvi, 792 pp.

Lederman, Minna [editor]. *Stravinsky in the Theatre.* New York: Pellegrini & Cudahy, 1949, 228 pp.

Lindlar, Heinrich. *Igor Strawinskys sakraler Gesang;* Geist und Form der Christkultischen Kompositionen. (Forschungsbeiträge zur Musikwissenschaft, 6.) Regensburg, G. Bosse, 1957, 93 pp.

Malipiero, Gian F. *Strawinsky.* Venice: Cavallino, 1945, 88 pp.

Monnikendam, Marius. *Strawinsky.* Haarlem: J. H. Gottmer, 1958, 222 pp.

Myers, Rollo: *Introduction to the Music of Stravinsky.* London: Dobson, 1950, 59 pp.

New York Public Library. *Stravinsky and the Dance.* A Survey of Ballet Productions 1910-1962. New York Public Library Dance Collection; [Distributed by Theatre Arts Books], New York, 1962, 60 pp.

Oleggini, Léon. *Connaissance de Stravinsky.* Lausanne: Foetisch, 1952, 228 pp.

Onnen, Frank. *Stravinsky.* Transl. from the Dutch by Mrs. M. M. Kessler-Button. Stockholm: Continental Book Co., 1949, 59 pp.

Paoli, Domenico de. *L'Opera di Strawinsky.* Milan, 1931, 160 pp.

Paoli, Domenico de. *Igor Strawinsky.* Nuovo ed. riveduta ed aggiornata. Turin: G. B. Paravia, 1934, 156 pp. (Previously publ. as *L'Opera di Strawinsky.*)

Ramuz, Charles F. *Souvenirs sur Igor Strawinsky.* Portraits et pages manuscrits. Lausanne: Mermod, 1946, 161 pp.

Ramuz, Charles F. *Souvenirs sur Igor Strawinsky.* Lausanne: Mermod, 1952, 137 pp.

Schaeffner, André. *Strawinsky.* Paris: Rieder, 1931, 127 pp.

Scharschuch, Horst. *Analyse zu Igor Strawinsky's "Sacre du Printemps."* (Forschungsbeiträge zur Musikwissenschaft, 8) Regensburg: Bosse, 1960, 25 pp.

Schloezer, Boris de. *Igor Stravinsky.* Paris: C. Aveline, 1929, 179 pp.

Siohan, Robert. *Stravinsky.* Bourges: Éditions du Seuil, 1959, 187 pp.

Sopeña, Federico. *Strawinsky; vida, obra y estilo.* Madrid: Sociedad de Estudios y Publicaciones, 1956, 270 pp.

Strawinsky, Théodore. *Le Message d'Igor Strawinsky.* Lausanne: F. Rouge, 1948, 127 pp.

Strawinsky, Théodore. *The Message of Igor Strawinsky.* Transl. by Robert Craft and Andre Marion. London, New York: Boosey & Hawkes, 1953, 57 pp.

Strobel, Heinrich. *Stravinsky: Classic Humanist.* Transl. by Hans Rosenwald. New York: Merlin Press, 1955, 184 pp.

Strobel, Heinrich. *Igor Strawinsky.* Zürich: Atlantis, 1956, 93 pp.

Stuckenschmidt, Hans H. *Strawinsky und sein Jahrhundert.* Berlin, Dahlem: Akademie der Künste, 1957, 51 pp.

Tansman, Alexandre. *Igor Stravinsky.* Paris: Amiot, Dumont, 1948, 314 pp.

Tansman, Alexandre. *Igor Stravinsky; The Man and His Music.* Transl. by Therese and Charles Bleefield. New York: Putnam, 1949, xv, 295 pp.

Tansman, Alexandre. *Igor Stravinsky.* Traducción de Roberto García Morillo. Buenos Aires: Editorial Argentina de Música, 1949, 242 pp.

Vlad, Roman. *Stravinsky.* Transl. by Frederick and Ann Fuller. London, New York: Oxford Univ. Press, 1960, 232 pp.

White, Eric W. *Stravinsky's Sacrifice to Apollo.* London: L. and Virginia Woolf at the Hogarth Press, 1930, vii, 9-150 pp.

White, Eric W. *Stravinsky; A Critical Survey.* New York: Philosophical Library, 1948, 192 pp.

White, Eric W. *Strawinsky.* Uebertragung: Gottfried von Einem. Hamburg: Claassen, 1949, 247 pp.

III. Periodical Articles Devoted to Stravinsky

Ansermet, Ernest. *Igor Stravinsky, The Man and His Work.* MC, LXXI/21 (1915), 41.

Ansermet, Ernest. *Einführung in das Schaffen Igor Strawinskys.* MdA, IV (1922), 169-72.

Ansermet, Ernest. *Strawinsky's Gift to the West.* DI, VI (1947), 235-36.

Asafiev, Boris. *Prozess der Formbildung bei Strawinsky.* A, IX (1929), 101-06.

Asafiev, Boris. *Über die Art des Einfluss Strawinskys auf die zeitgenössische Musik.* A, IX (1929), 106-08.

Auric, Georges. *Hommage à Igor Strawinsky.* RM, Numéro special (1939), pp. 333-34.

Babitz, Sol. *Igor Stravinsky's Rhythmic Innovations.* IM, XLVII (1949), 22, 36.

Balanchine, George. *The Dance Element in Strawinsky's Music.* DI, VI (1947), 250-56.

Balanchine, George. *Das Tänzerische Element.* MdZ, 12 (1955), 20-23.

Bayfield, Stanley. *Igor Stravinsky.* NMR, XXIV (1925), 396-98.

Beaumont, Cyril. *Some Memorable Occasions.* T, Summer 1948, 9-14.

Berger, Arthur. *Music for the Ballet.* DI, VI (1947), 258-77.

Berger, Arthur. *Stravinsky and His Firmament.* SR, XXXVII (1954), 58.

Berger, Arthur. *Stravinsky and the Younger American Composer.* S, 12 (1955), 38-46.

Berger, Arthur. *Stravinsky from the Source.* SR, XXXVIII (1955), 58-59.

Berger, Arthur. *Strawinsky und die Jungen.* MdZ, 12 (1955), 71-77.

Bernstein, Leonard. *A Note on Variety.* DI, VI (1947), 283.

Bernstein, Leonard, and Carlos Chávez, Aaron Copland, Alexei Haieff, Walter Piston, William Schuman. *Tribut an Strawinsky.* MdZ, 12 (1955), 78-83.

Bertrand, Paul. *Les Idées de M. Igor Stravinsky sur le disque et la radio.* Ml, XCVIII (1936), 139-40, 155-56, 187-88, 220.

Blitzstein, Marc. *The Phenomenon of Stravinsky.* MQ, XXI (1935), 330-47.

Boll, André. *L'Oeuvre du théâtre de Stravinsky.* RM, Numéro spécial (1939), pp. 347-53.

Boys, Henry. *Stravinsky: Critical Categories Needed for a Study of His Music.* S, 1 (1949), 3-12.

Boys, Henry. *Stravinsky: A Propos His Aesthetic.* S, 2 (1950), 61-64.

Boys, Henry. *Strawinsky: The Musical Materials.* S, 4 (1951), 11-18.

Browne, Andrew. *Aspects of Stravinsky's Work.* M & L, XI (1930), 360-66.

Bruyr, José. *En marge: Simple histoire d'une collaboration.* RM, Numéro special (1939), pp. 354-55.

Calvocoressi, M. D. *A Russian Composer of To-day.* MT, LII (1911), 511-12.

Carter, Elliott. *With the Dancers.* MM, XIV (1937) 237-39.

Cazden, Norman. *Humor in the Music of Stravinsky and Prokofiev.* S & S, XVIII (1954), 52-74.

Chandler, Theodore. *Stravinsky's Apologia.* MM, XX (1942), 17-22.

Chennevière, Rudhyar. *The Two Trends of Modern Music in Stravinsky's Works.* MQ, V (1919), 169-74.

Citkowitz, Israel. *Stravinsky and Schoenberg; A Note on Syntax and Sensibility.* JR, I/3 (1954), 17-20.

Cocteau, Jean. *Stravinsky dernière heure.* RM, V (1923), 142-44.

Cocteau, Jean. *Parisian Memoir.* DI, VI (1947), 238-40.

Cocteau, Jean. *Igor Stravinsky und das russische Ballett.* M, XV (1948), 268-71.

Coeuroy, André. *Stravinsky et nos poètes.* RM, V (1923), 148-54.

Coeuroy, André. *Picasso and Stravinsky.* MM, V/2 (1928), 3-8.

Copland, Aaron. *Influence, Problem, Tone.* DI, VI (1947), 249.

Cortot, Alfred. *Igor Strawinsky, le piano et les pianistes.* RM, Numéro spécial (1939), pp. 264-308.

Craft, Robert. *Strawinsky's Revisions.* C, 18 (1953), 14-16.

Craft, Robert. *Reihenkompositionen: vom "Septett" zum "Agon."* MdZ, 12 (1955), 43-54.

Craft, Robert. *Zwei Widmungen an Debussy.* MdZ, Neue Folge 1 (1958), 68-72.

Curjel, Hans. *Strawinsky oder die künstlerische Atmosphäre von Paris.* M, VIII (1929), 167-71.

Dahl, Ingolf. *Stravinsky in 1946.* MM, XXIII (1946), 159-65.

Dahl, Ingolf. *The New Orpheus.* DI, VI (1947), 285-86.

Döflein, Erich. *Über Strawinsky.* M, IV (1926), 158-60.

Drew, David. *Stravinsky's Revisions.* S, 20 (1957), 47-58.

Druckman, Jacob. *Stravinsky's Orchestral Style.* JR, IV/2 (1957), 10-19.

Druckman, Jacob. *Über den Orchesterstil.* MdZ, Neue Folge 1 (1958), 23-29.

Druskin, M. *Das Klavier in Igor Strawinskys Kunst.* A, IX (1929), 109-11.

Dushkin, Samuel. *Arbeit und Zusammenarbeit.* MdZ, Neue Folge 1 (1958), 81-86.

Evans, Edwin. *Igor Stravinsky: Contrapuntal Titan.* MA, XXXIII/16 (1921), 9.

Evans, Peter. *Stravinsky: Information and Illusion.* T, 57 (1961), pp. 2-5.

Ferroud, Pierre-Octave. *Das ästhetische Problem bei Strawinsky.* M, IX (1930), 365-70.

Ferroud, Pierre-Octave. *The Role of the Abstract in Igor Strawinsky's Work.* Ch, XI (1930), 141-47.

Fiechtner, Helmut. *Igor Strawinsky: seine Persönlichkeit und Kunstauffassung.* OM, III (1948), 70-74.

Fleisher, Herbert. *Rhythmische Veränderung durch Strawinskij.* Mk, XXIV (1932), 654-57.

Fox, Charles W. *Igor Strawinsky.* N, V (1948), 519-21.

Frankenstein, Alfred. *Stravinsky in Beverly Hills.* MM, XIX (1942), 178-81.

Frankenstein, Alfred. *The Record of a Self-Interpreter.* HF, VII/6 (1957), 42-43.

Friedland, Martin. *Igor Strawinskijs "Musikauffassung."* AMz, LVIII (1931), 849-51.

Gassman, Remi. *The New Stravinsky.* MM, XXVIII (1941), 114-16.

Gerhard, Roberto. *Twelve-Note Technique in Stravinsky.* S, 20 (1957), 38-43.

Gerhard, Roberto. *Die Reihentechnik des Diatonikers.* MdZ, Neue Folge 1 (1958), 18-22.

Goldschmidt, H. *Janáček und Strawinsky.* MG, IX (1959), 21-23.

Grohmann, Will. *Der Anteil der bildenden Kunst.* MdZ, Neue Folge 1 (1958), 43-50.

Haieff, Alexei. *The Artist and the Man.* DI, VI (1947), 237.

Henry, Leigh. *Igor Stravinsky.* MT, LX (1919), 268-72.

Henry, Leigh. *The Humor of Stravinsky.* MT, LX (1919), 670-73.

Henry, Leigh. *Igor Stravinsky and the Objective Direction in Contemporary Music.* Ch, n.ser.no.4 (1920), 97-102.

Henry, Leigh. *Stravinsky and the Pragmatic Criterion in Contemporary Music.* ER, XXXIII (1921), 67-73.

Heuss, Alfred. *Igor Strawinsky im Gewandhaus.* ZfM, XC (1923), 19-23.

Hill, Edward B. *A Note on Stravinsky.* HMR, II/7 (1914), 3-7, 23.

Hoérée, Arthur. *Invention pure et matière musicale chez Strawinsky.* RM, Numéro spécial (1939), pp. 340-43.

Honegger, Arthur. *Strawinsky, homme de métier.* RM, Numéro spécial (1939), pp. 261-63.

Hvad siger kollegerne? Udtalelser af danske komponisten (Dänische Komponisten über Igor Strawinsky). DM, XXVII (1952), 198-201.

Kalisch, Alfred. *Stravinsky Day by Day.* MT, LXIII (1922), 27-28.

Kall, Alexis. *Stravinsky in the Chair of Poetry.* MQ, XXVI (1940), 283-96.

Karsavina, Tamara. *A Recollection of Strawinsky.* T, Summer 1948, 7-9.

Keller, Hans. *Schönberg and Stravinsky: Schönbergians and Stravinskyans.* MR, XV (1954), 307-10.

Keller, Hans. *Rhythm: Gershwin and Stravinsky.* S, 20 (1957), 19-31.

Keller, Wilhelm. *Strawinskys Musik im Spiegel seiner "Poetik."* ZfM, CXIII (1952), 321.

Kirstein, Lincoln. *Working with Stravinsky.* MM, XIV (1937), 143-46.

Kirchmeyer, Hellmut. *Optisches und Analytisches zu Strawinskys Klaviersonaten.* MdZ, 12 (1955), 57-62.

Koegler, Horst. *Musik sichtbar gemacht: Strawinsky-Balanchine.* MdZ, 12 (1955), 24-29.

Lang, Paul H. *Stravinsky: the Enigma.* SR, XXX (1947), 36-37.

Lang, Paul H. *Fusillade from Stravinsky.* SR, XLII (1959), 50-51.

Landormy, Paul. *L'Art russe et Igor Stravinsky.* Mq, II (1929), 933-39.

Lederman, Minna. *Strawinsky's Theatre.* DI, VI (1947), 229-33.

Leduc, Jacques. *Les Écrits de Strawinsky.* CM, III/16 (1958), 37-43.

Leibowitz, René. *Igor Strawinsky, ou le choix de la misère musicale.* TM, I (1946), 1320-36.

Leibowitz, René. *Schönberg and Stravinsky.* PR, XV (1948), 361-65.

Levinson, André. *Stravinsky et la danse.* RM, V (1923), 155-65.

Lewkovitch, B. *Interviews med Stravinsky.* DM, XXXIV (1959), 145-49.

Lewkovitch, B. *Igor Strawinskij igen.* DM, XXV (1960), 242-43.

Lifar, Serge. *Igor Strawinsky; Législateur au ballet.* RM, Numéro spécial (1939), pp. 321-30.

Lifar, Serge. *Strawinsky et Diaghilev.* CM, III/16 (1958), 23-30.

Lindlar, Heinrich. *Der schöpferische Universalist.* Ma, II (1957), 311-14.

Lindlar, Heinrich. *Der Sakralkomponist.* MdZ, Neue Folge I (1958), 59-68.

Lourié, Arthur. *Neo-Gothic and Neo-Classic.* MM, V/3 (1928), 3-8.

Mason, Colin. *Strawinsky's Contributions to Chamber Music.* T, 43 (1957), 6-16.

Mason, Colin. *Die Kammermusik.* MdZ, Neue Folge I (1958), 72-81.

Manuel, Roland. *Stravinsky et la critique.* RP, 9 (1924), 17-18.

Manuel, Roland. *Démarche de Strawinsky.* RM, Numéro spécial (1939), pp. 255-60.

Menasce, Jacques de. *Anniversary of Igor Stravinsky.* JR, IV/2 (1956-57), 3-9.

Messiaen, Olivier. *Le Rythme chez Igor Strawinsky.* RM, Numéro spécial (1939), pp. 331-32.

Milhaud, Darius. *A propos d'une première audition d'Igor Strawinsky.* RM, Numéro spécial (1939), p. 309.

Milhaud, Darius. *Thirty-seven Years.* DI, VI (1947), 257.

Milner, A. *Melody in Stravinsky's Music.* MT, XCVIII (1957), 370-71.

Mitchell, D. *Bartók, Stravinsky and Schoenberg. Periods: Early, Middle and Late.* Ch, XXVIII (1953), 9-16.

Mitchell, Edward. *The Stravinsky Theories.* MT, LXIII (1922), 162-64.

Monteux, Pierre. *Early Years.* DI, VI (1947), 242-43.

Murrill, H. *Stravinsky To-day.* Ch, XXIII (1949), 85-91.

Murrill, H. *Aspects of Stravinsky.* M&L, XXXII (1951), 118-24.

Myers, Rollo. *Stravinsky at Seventy-five.* MT, XCVIII (1957), 313-14.

Nabokov, Nicolas. *Stravinsky Now.* PR, XI (1944), 324-34.

Nabokov, Nicolas. *Strawinsky, 1947.* St, I (1947), 6-12.

Nabokov, Nicolas. *The Atonal Trail: A Communication.* PR, XV (1948), 580-85.

Nabokov, Nicolas. *Atonality and Obscurantism.* PR, XV (1948), 1148-51.

Nabokov, Nicolas. *Igor Stravinsky.* AM, 184 (1949), 21-27.

Nabokov, Nicolas. *Christmas 1949 mit Strawinsky.* MdZ, 12 (1955), 5-19.

Pannain, Guido. *Igor Stravinsky.* RaM, I. (1928), 281-96.

Perrin, Maurice. *Stravinsky in a Composition Class.* S, 20 (1957), 44-46.

Perrin, Maurice. *Lehrer Strawinsky.* MdZ, Neue Folge I (1958), 86-87.

Petit, Raymond. *A Critical Portrait of Stravinsky.* MM, VII (1930), 37-41.

Piston, Walter. *Strawinsky's Re-discoveries.* DI, VI (1947), 256-57.

Pringsheim, Heinz. *Aus Strawinskijs Falschmünzerwerkstatt.* AM-Z, LI (1924), 939.

Ramuz, C. F. *Erinnerungen an Igor Strawinsky.* SM, LXIX (1929), 1-8.

Ramuz, C. F. *Erinnerungen an Strawinsky.* M, XXI (1954), 129-31.

Ramuz, C. F. *Deux images du compositeur.* CM, III/16 (1958), 44-46.

Raynor, H. *Stravinsky the Teacher.* Ch, XXXI (1956), 35-41, 69-75.

Regner, O. F. *Der Weg zum "reinen" Tanz.* MdZ, Neue Folge I (1958), 35-42.

Rennert, G. *Strawinsky's Conception of Opera.* O, VII (1956), 473-74.

Rieti, Vittorio. *The Composer's Debt.* DI, VI (1947), 278.

Rosenfeld, Paul. *Stravinsky.* NR, XXII (1920), 207-10.

Rosenfeld, Paul. *Igor Strawinskij.* MdA, III (1921), 191-95.

Rosenfeld, Paul. *Stravinsky.* NR, LXX (1932), 128-29.

Rutz, Hans. *Strawinsky und die Zukunft der Oper.* OM, VII (1952), 213-18.

Sabaneev, Leonid. *The Stravinsky Legends.* MT, LXIX (1928), 785-87.

Saminsky, Lazare. *Mediterranean Stravinsky — A New Myth.* MM, X (1932), 137-38.

Schaeffner, André. *On Stravinsky, Early and Late.* MM, XII (1934), 3-7.

Schaeffner, André. *Critique et thématique.* RM, Numéro spécial (1939), pp. 241-54.

Scherber, Ferdinand. *Ein Interview oder Igor Strawinskys Kritik an der Kritik.* Sig, LXXXVII (1929), 408-09.

Schloezer, Boris de. *Igor Stravinsky.* RM, V (1923), 92-141.

Schloezer, Boris de. *Igor Stravinsky und Serge Prokofjeff.* M, IV (1925), 469-81.

Schloezer, Boris de. *Sur Strawinsky.* RM, X/4 (1929), 1-19.

Schloezer, Boris de. *The Enigma of Stravinsky.* MM, X (1931), 10-17.

Schloezer, Boris de. *L'Enigma di Stravinsky.* RaM, VII (1934), 89-96.

Schmidt-Garre, Helmut. *Igor Stravinsky.* NMZ, II/2 (1948), 38-46.

Schoen, Ernst. *Über Strawinskys Einfluss.* M, VIII (1929), 162-66.

Schoenewolf, Karl. *Gespräch mit Strawinskij.* Mk, XXI (1929), 499-503.

Schubert, Reinhold. *Einige Bemerkungen zum Thema.* MdZ, Neue Folge I (1958), 5-11.

Schuh, Willi. *Zur Harmonik Igor Strawinskys.* SM, XCII (1952), 243-52.

Schuh, Willi. *Strawinsky und die Tradition.* M, XXIII (1956), 308-13.

Schulhoff, Erwin. *Paraphrase über Herrn Strawinsky.* A, IV (1924), 281-83.

Schuman, William. *The Final Triumph.* DI, VI (1947), 282-83.

Schumann, Karl. *Ein Antiliterat und die Literatur.* MdZ, Neue Folge I (1958), 50-59.

Sessions, Roger. *Thoughts on Stravinsky.* S, 20 (1957), 32-37.

Slonimsky, Nicolas. *Centenario de Strawinsky,* Nueva York, junio de 1982; fidel y verdadera anticipación del dia en que el maquinismo glorifique la música. Mia, IV/15-16 (1931), 3-8.

Smith, Moses. *Stravinsky Meets the Boston Censor.* MM, XXI (1944), 171-72.

Souvtchinsky, Pierre. *La Notion du temps et la musique.* RM, Numéro spécial (1939), pp. 310-20.

Souvtchinsky, Pierre. *Igor Stravinsky.* Co, 2 (1946), 19-31.

Souvtchinsky, Pierre. *Qui est Strawinsky?* CM, III/16 (1958), 7-14.

Souvtchinsky, Pierre. *Zeit und Musik.* MdZ, Neue Folge I (1958), 12-18.

Stefan, Paul. *Strawinsky-Memoiren.* MdA, XVIII (1936), 17-19.

Steinhard, Erich. *Igor Strawinskij.* Mk, XXIII (1931), 574-77.

Stockhausen, Karlheinz. *Musik in Funktion.* M, XXIV (1957), 249-51.

Strobel, Heinrich. *Strawinskys Weg.* M, VIII (1929), 158-62.

Strobel, Heinrich. *Strawinsky privat.* M, X (1931), 315-18.

Strobel, Heinrich. *Igor Strawinsky.* M, XIV (1947), 328-32, 377-79.

Strobel, Heinrich. *Les Oeuvres récentes de Strawinsky.* CM, III/16 (1958), 31-35.

Struth, Sigrid. *Klassiche Symphonik.* MdZ, 12 (1955), 63-68.

Stuart, Charles. *Recent Works Examined.* T, Summer 1948, 20-28.

Stuart, Charles. *Stravinsky: the Dialectics of Dislike,* MS, II (1950), 142-48.

Stuckenschmidt, H. H. *Strawinsky oder die Vereinigung des Unvereinbaren.* MdA, XIV (1932), 67-70.

Stuckenschmidt, H. H. *Die Ballettpartituren.* MdZ, Neue Folge I (1958), 30-35.

Tiby, Ottavio. *Igor Strawinsky.* P, V (1924), 216-22.

Verbitsky, Bernardo. *Algo sobre Strawinsky.* Nos, II (1937), 180-90.

Vermeulen, Matthijs. *Rondom Stravinsky.* Muz, II (1927), 1-12.

Vlad, Roman. *Le Musiche sacre de Strawinsky.* RaM, XXII (1952), 212-19.

Vlad, Roman. *Esordi di Strawinsky.* RaM, XXVI (1956), 100-05.

Vuillermoz, Emile. *Igor Stravinsky.* RM, VIII/5 (1912), 15-21.

Weissmann, Adolf. *Strawinsky.* MdA, VI (1924), 228-34.

Weissmann, Adolf. *Igor Strawinsky.* BdS, V/8 (1925), 2-6.

Wellesz, Egon. *Strawinsky.* A, II (1922), 39-41.

Weterings, J. *Stravinsky*. RMB, III/8 (1927), 1-4.

Weterings, J. *Au sujet de Stravinsky*. RMB, VI/14 (1930), 1-2.

Wise, C. Stanley. *Impressions of Igor Strawinsky*. MQ, II (1916), 249-56.

IV. REFERENCES TO SPECIFIC WORKS IN PERIODICALS

Agon

Helm, E. *Donaueschingen 1957*. MT, XCVIII (1957), 688-89.

Keller, Hans. *Strawinsky's Performance of "Agon"; A Report*. T, 50 (1959), 22-25.

Morton, Lawrence. *Current Chronicle: Los Angeles*. MQ, XLIII (1957), 535-41.

Reich, Willi. *Donaueschinger Musiktage 1957*. SM, XCVII (1957), 497.

Apollon Musagètes

Gutman, Hanns. *Strawinsky: Apollo Musagètes*. A, VIII (1928), 224-25.

Hammond, Richard. *Ballets Russes, 1928*. MM, VI/1 (1928), 25-28.

Jacobi, Frederick. *The New Apollo*. MM, V/4 (1928), 11-15.

Lederman, Minna. *With the Dancers*. MM, XXIII (1946), 71.

Lourié, Arthur. *À propos de l'Apollon d'Igor Strawinsky*. Mq, I/3 (1928), 117-19.

Lourié, Arthur. *Stravinsky's "Apollo."* D, I/10 (1928), 20-21.

Redlich, Hans F. *Strawinskys "Apollon Musagètes."* MdA, XI (1929), 41-44.

Sabaneev, Leonid. *Dawn or Dusk? Strawinsky's New Ballets: "Apollo" and "The Fairy Kiss."* MT, LXX (1929), 403-06.

Schloezer, Boris de. *Apollon Musagètes*. MO, XI (1929), 8-12.

Strobel, Heinrich. *Vom Apollon zur Psalmensinfonie*. M, X (1931), 219-24.

Le Baiser de la fée

Lederman, Minna. *With the Dancers*. MM, XXIII (1946), 137-38.

Mangeot, A. *Les Ballets de Mme. Ida Rubinstein*. MMu, XXXIX (1928), 413.

Manuel, Roland. *Le Baiser de la fée*. Mq, II (1928), 657-59.

Prunières, Henry. *Stravinsky and Ravel, Winter 1928*. MM, VI/2 (1929), 35-39.

Canticum sacrum ad honorem Sancti Marci nominis

Brindle, R. S. *The Venice International Festival of Contemporary Music*. MT, XCVII (1956), 599.

Schuh, W. *Strawinskys "Canticum Sacrum . . ."* MK, XXVI (1956), 296-98.

Stein, Erwin. *Igor Strawinsky's Canticum Sacrum ad Honorem S. Marci Nominis*. T, 40 (1956), 3-5.

Stuckenschmidt, H. *Höhepunkt der Biennale: Strawinskys Canticum sacrum*. M, XXIII (1956), 293-94.

Weissmann, J. S. *Current Chronicle: Italy*. MQ, XLIII (1957), 104-10.

Capriccio

Lapommeraye, Pierre de. *Capriccio, Paris, Salle Pleyel, Dec. 6, 1929*. Ml, XCI (1929), 537.

Lourié, Arthur. *Le Capriccio de Strawinsky*. RM, XI (1930), 353-55.

Schaeffner, André. *Stravinsky's "Capriccio."* MM, VII/2 (1930), 31-34.

L'Histoire du soldat

Ansermet, Ernest. *L'Histoire du Soldat.* Ch, n. ser. no. 10 (1920), 289-95.

Meadmore, W. S. *Stravinsky's "The Soldier's Tale."* MSt, XXX/518 (1927), 38-39.

Schnoor, Hans. *Strawinsky's "Geschichte vom Soldaten."* A, IV (1924), 276-80.

Jeu de cartes

Denby, Edwin. *With the Dancers.* MM, XVIII (1940), 61-63.

Thompson, Oscar. *New Stravinsky Ballet Achieves World Première.* MA, LVII/9 (1937), 19.

Mavra

Jacobi, Frederick. *Reflections on Ariadne and Mavra.* MM, XII (1935), 73-78.

"Mavra" Reveals New Stravinsky to Paris. MA, XXXVI/10 (1922), 10.

Milhaud, Darius. *Strawinskys neue Bühnenwerke.* MdA, IV (1922), 260-62.

Thompson, Oscar. *Stravinsky's Mavra is Introduced by Philadelphians.* MA, LV/1 (1935), 3, 7.

Les Noces

Casella, Alfredo. *Stravinsky's Noces Villageoises.* Ar, IX/2 (1926), 73-75.

Castelnuovo-Tedesco, Mario. *Leggendo "Les Noces" di Strawinski.* P, VIII (1927), 15-25.

Gray, Cecil. *The Music of Les Noces.* NA, XXXIX (1926), 416.

Hammond, Richard. *Viewing "Les Noces" in 1929.* MM, VI/3 (1929), 19-25.

Manuel, Roland. *Igor Stravinsky's "Les Noces."* Ch, n. ser. no. 33 (1923), 1-4.

Ramuz, C. F. *Souvenir of Switzerland — 1917.* DI, VI (1947), 245-48.

Schaeffner, André. *Ballets Russes: Noces d'Igor Strawinsky.* Ml, LXXXV (1923), 287-88.

Stokowski, Leopold. *Concerning Stravinsky's "Les Noces."* MC, XCVIII/16 (1929), 24.

Vuillermoz, Emile. *Chroniques et notes . . . Noces: Igor Strawinsky.* RM, IV/10 (1923), 69-72.

Oedipus Rex

Copland, Aaron. *Stravinsky's Oedipus Rex.* NR, LIV (1928), 68-69.

Henry, Leigh. *Oedipus Rex and the Objective Music Drama.* MC, CIII/5 (1931), 7, 10.

Lourié, Arthur. *"Oedipus Rex" de Stravinsky.* RM, VIII/8 (1927), 240-53.

Lourié, Arthur. *Oedipus Rex. Opern-Oratorium nach Sophokles von Igor Strawinsky.* BdS, VIII/19 (1928), 9-13.

Mersmann, Hans. *Strawinsky: "Oedipus Rex"; zur Frage der Antikenoper* von Hans Mersmann, Hans Schultze-Ritter, H. Strobel, und Lothar Windsperger. M, VII (1928), 180-83.

Oedipus Rex. MMu, XXXVIII (1927), 325-26.

Rosenfeld, Paul. *Oedipus Rex, Cocteau and Stravinsky.* NR, LXVI (1931), 356-57.

Sabaneeff, Leonid. *Stravinsky's "Oedipus."* Ch, VIII (1927), 258-61.

Schloezer, Boris de. *L'Oedipus Rex de Stravinsky.* RP, 45 (1927), 291-93.

Sessions, Roger. *On Oedipus Rex.* MM, V/3 (1928), 9-15.

Strobel, Heinrich. *Strawinskys Neuklassizismus: "Oedipus Rex" in Berlin.* NM-Z, XLIX (1928), 433-37.

L'Oiseau de feu

Dennington, A. *The Three Orchestrations of Stravinsky's "Firebird."* Ch, 34 (1960), 89-94.

Evans, Edwin. *The Music of L'Oiseau de Feu.* DT, July 1939, 400-01.

Perséphone

Chantavoine, Jean. *Ballets de Mme. Rubinstein: Perséphone de MM André Gide et Strawinsky.* Ml, XCVI (1934), 178-79.

Jacobi, Frederick. *On Hearing Stravinsky's "Perséphone."* MM, XII/3 (1935), 112-15.

Mangeot, A. *Les Ballets de Mme. Ida Rubinstein: Perséphone.* MMu, XLV (1934), 147-50.

Seroff, Victor. *Gide and Stravinsky; Perséphone.* SR, XL/48 (1957), 49.

Petrushka

Boys, Henry. *Note on the New "Pétrouchka."* T, Summer 1948, 15-18.

Diaghileff Ballet Introduces "Pétrouchka." MA, XXIII/13 (1916), 3-4.

Rivière, Jacques. *Pétrouchka, ballet d'Igor Strawinsky.* NRF, III (1911), 376-77.

Schaeffner, André. *Pétrouchka.* Ml, XCIII (1931), 241-44.

Sternfeld, Frederick. *Some Russian Folksongs in Stravinsky's "Petrushka."* N, II (1945), 95-119.

Pulcinella

Chop, Max. *Strawinsky-Abend in der Staatsoper.* Sig, LXXXIII (1925), 1055-57.

Roussy de Sales, Raoul de. *Igor Stravinsky's "Pulcinella."* Ch, n. ser. no. 8 (1920), 234-36.

Salazar, Adolfo. *Pulcinella and Maese Pedro.* Ch, VI (1925), 119-25.

Le Chant du rossignol

Calvocoressi, M. D. M. *Igor Stravinsky's Opera "The Nightingale."* MT, LV (1914), 372-74.

Chantavoine, Jean. *Igor Stravinsky's "Rossignol"* Sig, LXXII (1914), 939-41.

Prunières, Henry. *Igor Stravinsky's "Chant du Rossignol."* Ch, n. ser. no. 9 (1920), 271-74.

The Rake's Progress

Levinger, H. W. *Stravinsky's "The Rake's Progress" in U. S. Première.* MC, CXLVII/5 (1953), 6-7.

Murrill, Herbert. *The Rake's Progress.* S, 6 (1952), 55-58.

Le Sacre du printemps

Chávez, Carlos. *The Surprise and the Scandal.* DI, VI (1947), 243-44.

Petzold, Friedrich. *Formbildende Rhythmik zu Strawinskys "Sacre du Printemps."* M, XX (1953), 46-47.

Lalo, Pierre. *Remarks on the Ballet "Le Sacre du Printemps."* NMR, II (1913), 440-42.

Mangeot, A. *Le Sacre du Printemps.* MMu, XXV/II (1913), 176.

Rivière, Jacques. *Le Sacre du Printemps.* NRF, V (1913), 706-30.

Schaeffner, André. *Storia e significato del "Sacre du Printemps" di Strawinsky.* RaM, II (1929), 536-51.

Travis, R. *Towards A New Concept of Tonality?* JMT, III (1959), 257-94.

Vuillermoz, Emile. *Le Sacre du Printemps.* RM, II/4 (1921), 161-64.

Vuillermoz, Emile. *La Saison russe au Théâtre des Champs-Elysées: La Sacre.* SIM, 1913, 52-56.

Symphonie de psaumes

Piston, Walter. *Stravinsky as Psalmist — 1931.* MM, VIII/2 (1931), 42-45.

Prunières, Henry. *Symphonie de Psaumes d'Igor Strawinsky.* RM, XII (1931), 79-81.

Threni, id est lamentatione Jeremiae prophetae

Daniel, Oliver. *Twelve-Tone Stravinsky.* SR, XLII/42 (1959), 84.

Mila, M. *Venezia.* RaM, XXVIII (1958), 215-17.

Pauli, Hansjörg. *On Strawinsky's "Threni."* T, 49 (1958), 16-32.

Weissmann, J. S. *Current Chronicle: Italy.* MQ, XLV (1959), 104-10.

Other Works

Babitz, Sol. *Stravinsky's Symphony in C — 1940.* MQ, XXVII (1941), 20-25.

Craft, Robert. *A Note on Gesualdo's "Sacrae Cantiones" and on Gesualdo and Strawinsky.* T, 45 (1957), 5-7.

Eimert, Herbert. *Die Drei Shakespeare-Lieder — 1953.* MdZ, 12 (1955), 35-38.

Garbutt, John, and Matthew Patterson. *An Approach to Stravinsky's "Cantata" and "The Wedding."* M&L, XXXVIII (1957), 28-31.

Goldman, R. F. *Current Chronicle: New York.* MQ, XXV (1949), 451-58.

Gutman, Hanns. *Strawinsky, alt und neu; Uraufführung seines Violinkonzertes.* A, XI (1931), 278-79.

Keller, Hans. *In Memoriam Dylan Thomas: Strawinskys Schönbergische Technik.* MdZ, 12 (1955), 39-42.

Keller, Hans. *Stravinsky's Schoenbergian Technique.* T, 35 (1955), 13-20.

Lindlar, Heinrich. *Igor Strawinskys "Cantata."* SM, XCIII (1953), 397-401.

Lindlar, Heinrich. *Cantata.* MdZ, 12 (1955), 30-34.

Lindlar, Heinrich. *Ebony Concerto.* MdZ, 12 (1955), 69-70.

Lourié, Arthur. *La Sonate de Stravinsky.* RM, VI/10 (1925), 100-04.

Mason, Colin. *Strawinsky's Newest Works.* T, 54 (1960), 2-10.

Mason, Colin. *Strawinsky's New Work (A Sermon, A Narrative and A Prayer),* T, 59 (1961), 5-14.

Prunières, Henry. *Le Concerto en ré majeur, pour violon et orchestre, de Strawinsky.* RM, XIII/122 (1932), 59-60.

Schilling, H. L. *Igor Strawinskys Erweiterung und Instrumentation der Canonischen Orgelvariationen "Von Himmel hoch, da komm ich her" von J. S. Bach.* MK, XXVII (1957), 257-75.

Schloezer, Boris de. *À propos de la Sonate de Strawinsky.* RP, 26 (1925), 18-20.

Schuh, Willi. *Das Basler Concerto.* MdZ, 12 (1955), 55-56.

Strobel, Heinrich. *Strawinskys Violinkonzert.* M, X (1931), 377-79.

Strobel, Heinrich. *Strawinskys "Symphony in Three Movements."* M, XV (1948), 271-76.

Tangeman, Robert. *Stravinsky's Two-Piano Works.* MM, XXII (1945), 93-98.

Weissmann, Adolf. *Strawinsky spielt sein Klavierkonzert.* MdA, VI (1924), 407-09.

A complete

LIST OF WORKS

PIANO SOLO

Quatre Études pour piano, Op. 7 (1908)
Rob. Forberg—A. Jurgenson

Piano-Rag Music (1919)
J. and W. Chester

Les Cinq doigts (1921)
　Eight very easy pieces on five notes for piano
J. and W. Chester

Sonata for Piano (1924)
Édition Russe de Musique (S. et N. Koussewitzky)—Boosey and Hawkes

Serenade in A (1925)
Édition Russe de Musique (S. et N. Koussewitzky)—Boosey and Hawkes

Tango (1940)
Mercury—B. Schotts Söhne
　Orchestral version
B. Schotts Söhne

PIANO DUET

Three Easy Pieces *(Trois Pièces faciles)* (1915)
　For piano duet (easy left hand)
J. and W. Chester

Five Easy Pieces *(Cinq Pièces faciles)* (1917)
　For piano duet (easy right hand)
J. and W. Chester

Two Pianos

Concerto for Two Solo Pianos (1935)
B. Schotts Söhne
Paris, Nov. 21, 1935, Igor and Soulima Stravinsky

Sonata for Two Pianos (1944)
B. Schotts Söhne
Madison, Wis., July 1944, Nadia Boulanger and Richard Johnson

Violin or Viola

Elégie (1944)
B. Schotts Söhne
New York, 1946

Violin and Piano

Duo concertant (1932)
Édition Russe de Musique (S. et N. Koussewitzky)—Boosey and Hawkes
Berlin (radio). Oct. 28, 1932

Clarinet

Three Pieces for Clarinet Solo (1919)
J. and W. Chester
Lausanne, Nov. 8, 1918, Edmond Allegra

Chamber Music

Three Pieces for String Quartet (1914)
Édition Russe de Musique (S. et N. Koussewitzky)—Boosey and Hawkes

Ragtime (1918)
  For eleven instruments
J. and W. Chester
Paris, 1925, cond. Stravinsky

Concertino (1920)
  For string quartet
W. Hansen
New York, Nov. 23, 1920, Flonzaley Quartet

Octet for Wind Instruments (1923, rev. 1952)
Édition Russe de Musique (S. et N. Koussewitzky)—Boosey and Hawkes
Paris, Oct. 18, 1923, cond. Stravinsky

Septet (1953)
   For clarinet, horn, bassoon, piano, violin, viola, and cello
Boosey and Hawkes
Washington, D.C., Jan. 24, 1954

Epitaphium (1959)
Für das Grabmal des Prinzen zu Fürstenberg
   For flute, clarinet, and harp
Boosey and Hawkes
Donaueschingen, Oct. 17, 1959

Double Canon, *Raoul Dufy in Memoriam* (1959)
   For two violins, viola, and cello
Boosey and Hawkes
New York, Dec. 20, 1959

DANCE BAND

Ebony Concerto (1945)
Charling Music Corp.
New York, Mar. 25, 1946, Woody Herman's Band, cond. Walter Hendl

SOLO VOICE WITH INSTRUMENTAL ACCOMPANIMENT

Le Faune et la bergère, Op. 2 (1905-06)
   Suite for voice and piano. Words by A. Pushkin
M. P. Belaieff
St. Petersburg, Feb. 29, 1908

Deux Mélodies, Op. 6 (1907)
   For mezzo-soprano and piano. Words by S. Gorodetzky
Rob. Forberg—A. Jurgenson
St. Petersburg, 1908

Pastorale (1908)
   Song without words for soprano and piano
Rob. Forberg—A. Jurgenson—B. Schotts Söhne
St. Petersburg, 1908

Two Poems of Verlaine, Op. 9 (1910)
   For baritone and piano
Boosey and Hawkes

Two Poems by K. Balmont (1911, rev. 1947)
    For high voice and piano
Édition Russe de Musique (S. et N. Koussewitzky)—Boosey and Hawkes

Trois Poésies de la lyrique japonaise (Three Japanese Lyrics) (1913)
    For high voice and piano
Boosey and Hawkes

Trois petites chansons (Souvenirs de mon enfance) (1913)
    For voice and piano
Édition Russe de Musique (S. et N. Koussewitzky)—Boosey and Hawkes

Pribaoutki (1914)
    Pleasant songs for medium voice and eight instruments
J. and W. Chester
Paris, 1919

Berceuses du chat (1915-16)
    For medium voice and three clarinets. Russian folk texts translated into
        French by C. F. Ramuz
J. and W. Chester

Trois Histoires pour enfants (1915-17)
    For voice and piano
J. and W. Chester

Quatre Chants russes (Four Russian Songs) (1918)
    For voice and piano
J. and W. Chester

Three Songs from William Shakespeare (1953)
    For mezzo-soprano, flute, clarinet, and viola
Boosey and Hawkes
Los Angeles, March 8, 1954

In Memoriam Dylan Thomas (1954)
    For tenor voice, string quartet, and four trombones
Boosey and Hawkes
Hollywood, Sept. 20, 1954

Four Russian Songs (1954)
    For voice, flute, harp, and guitar
J. and W. Chester

CHORUS UNACCOMPANIED

Four Russian Peasant Songs (1914-17)
For equal voices, unaccompanied
With an accompaniment of four horns (1954)
J. and W. Chester

Paternoster (1926)
For mixed chorus unaccompanied
Édition Russe de Musique (S. et N. Koussewitzky) — Boosey and Hawkes

Credo (1932)
For mixed chorus unaccompanied
Édition Russe de Musique (S. et N. Koussewitzky) — Boosey and Hawkes

Ave Maria (1934)
For mixed chorus unaccompanied
Édition Russe de Musique (S. et N. Koussewitzky) — Boosey and Hawkes

Anthem (1962)
The Dove Descending Breaks the Air
For chorus a cappella. Words by T. S. Eliot
Boosey and Hawkes
Los Angeles, Feb. 19, 1962

CHORAL WORKS

Le Roi des étoiles (1911)
Cantata for men's chorus and orchestra. Poem by K. Balmont
Rob. Forberg—A. Jurgenson
Brussels, 1938

Symphony of Psalms (Symphonie de Psaumes) (1930, rev. 1948)
For chorus and orchestra
Édition Russe de Musique (S. et N. Koussewitzky) — Boosey and Hawkes
Brussels, Dec. 13, 1960, cond. Ernest Ansermet

Babel (1944)
Cantata for male chorus, orchestra and narrator
B. Schotts Söhne
Los Angeles, 1945, cond. Werner Janssen

Mass (1948)
> For mixed chorus and double wind quintet
Boosey and Hawkes
Milan, Oct. 26, 1948, cond. Ernest Ansermet

Cantata (1952)
> For soprano, tenor, female chorus, and a small instrumental ensemble
Boosey and Hawkes
Los Angeles, Nov. 11, 1952, cond. Stravinsky

J. S. Bach: *Choral-Variationen über des Weihnachtslied 'Vom Himmel hoch da komm ich her'* (1956)
> For chorus and orchestra
Boosey and Hawkes
Ojai, Calif., May 27, 1956

Canticum sacrum (1956)
> For tenor and baritone soli, chorus, and orchestra
Boosey and Hawkes
Venice, Sept. 13, 1956, cond. Stravinsky

Threni; id est, Lamentationes Jeremiae Prophetae (1958)
> For soli, mixed chorus, and orchestra
Boosey and Hawkes
Venice, Sept. 23, 1958

A Sermon, A Narrative and a Prayer (1960-61)
> For chorus and orchestra
Boosey and Hawkes
Basle, Feb. 23, 1962, cond. Paul Sacher

CONCERTOS

Concerto for Piano and Wind Orchestra (1924)
Édition Russe de Musique (S. et N. Koussewitzky)—Boosey and Hawkes
Paris, May 22, 1924, cond. Serge Koussevitzky, soloist Stravinsky

Capriccio for Piano and Orchestra (1929)
Édition Russe de Musique (S. et N. Koussewitzky)—Boosey and Hawkes
Paris, Dec. 6, 1929, cond. Ernest Ansermet, soloist Stravinsky

Concerto in D for Violin and Orchestra (1931)
B. Schotts Söhne
Berlin, Oct. 23, 1931, cond. Stravinsky, soloist Samuel Dushkin

Movements (1948-59)
   For piano and orchestra
Boosey and Hawkes
New York, Jan. 10, 1960, soloist Margrit Weber

Symphonic Works

Symphony in E-flat, Op. 1 (1905-07)
Rob. Forberg—A. Jurgenson
St. Petersburg, Jan. 22, 1908

Scherzo fantastique, Op. 3 (1908)
B. Schotts Söhne
St. Petersburg, Feb. 6, 1909, cond. Alexander Siloti

Fireworks (Feu d'artifice), Op. 4 (1908)
   Fantasy for orchestra
B. Schotts Söhne
St. Petersburg, June 17, 1908, cond. Alexander Siloti

Chant des bateliers du Volga (Song of the Volga Boatmen) (1917)
   Russian folk song arranged for wind instruments and percussion
J. and W. Chester

Le Chant du rossignol (The Song of the Nightingale) (1917)
   Poème symphonique
Édition Russe de Musique (S. et N. Koussewitzky)—Boosey and Hawkes
Geneva, Dec. 6, 1919, cond. Ernest Ansermet

Suite No. 1 pour petit orchestre (1917-25)
J. and W. Chester
Milan, June 17, 1926

Symphonies of Wind Instruments (1920)
Édition Russe de Musique (S. et N. Koussewitzky)—Boosey and Hawkes
London, June 10, 1921, cond. Serge Koussevitzky
Revised version (1947) over NBC, 1948, cond. Ernest Ansermet

Suite No. 2, pour petit orchestre (1921)
J. and W. Chester
London, June 8, 1922, cond. Eugene Goossens

Quatre Études pour orchestre (Four Studies for Orchestra) (1929)
Édition Russe de Musique (S. et N. Koussewitzky)—Boosey and Hawkes
Berlin, Nov. 7, 1930, cond. Ernest Ansermet

Concerto in E-flat, *Dumbarton Oaks* (1938)
    For chamber orchestra
B. Schotts Söhne
Washington, D. C., May 8, 1938, cond. Nadia Boulanger

Symphonie en ut (C) (1940)
    In four movements
B. Schotts Söhne
Chicago, Nov. 7, 1940, cond. Stravinsky

Star-Spangled Banner (National Anthem) (1941)
Mercury
Los Angeles, Oct. 14, 1941, cond. James Sample

Danses concertantes (1941-42)
    For chamber orchestra
B. Schotts Söhne
Los Angeles, Feb. 8, 1942, cond. Stravinsky

Four Norwegian Moods (1942)
    For orchestra
B. Schotts Söhne
Boston, Jan. 1944, cond. Stravinsky

Circus Polka (1942)
    Composed for a young elephant
B. Schotts Söhne
New York, Spring 1942, Barnum & Bailey Circus

Ode (1943)
    Elegiacal chant in three parts
B. Schotts Söhne
Boston, Oct. 1943, cond. Serge Koussevitzky

Scherzo à la russe (1944)
B. Schotts Söhne
San Francisco, Mar. 22, 1946, cond. Stravinsky

Scènes de ballet (1944)
    For orchestra
B. Schotts Söhne
New York, 1944, cond. Maurice Abravanel

Symphony in Three Movements (1945)
B. Schotts Söhne
New York, Jan. 24, 1946, cond. Stravinsky

Concerto in D (*Basle Concerto*) (1946)
   For string orchestra
Boosey and Hawkes
Basle, Jan. 21, 1947, cond. Paul Sacher

Greeting Prelude (1955) For the 80th birthday of Pierre Monteux
   For orchestra
Boosey and Hawkes
Boston, April 4, 1955, cond. Charles Munch

Monumentum pro Gesualdo di Venosa ad CD annum (1960)
   For orchestra
Boosey and Hawkes
Venice, Sept. 1960, cond. Stravinsky

OPERAS, BALLETS, AND OTHER STAGE WORKS

L'Oiseau de feu (The Firebird) (1909-10)
   Revision 1945
B. Schotts Söhne
Paris, June 25, 1910, cond. Gabriel Pierné
   Suite for Orchestra (1911)
   Revisions 1919, 1945
J. and W. Chester (1920)

Le Rossignol (The Nightingale) (1909-14)
   Lyric tale in three acts after H. C. Andersen by Igor Stravinsky and S. Mitousoff
Édition Russe de Musique (S. et N. Koussewitzky)—Boosey and Hawkes
Paris, May 26, 1914, cond. Emile Cooper

Pétrouchka (1910-11)
   Burlesque in four scenes by Igor Stravinsky and Alexander Benois
Paris, June 13, 1911, cond. Pierre Monteux
   Suite du Ballet
Édition Russe de Musique (S. et N. Koussewitzky)—Boosey and Hawkes

The Rite of Spring (*Le Sacre du printemps*) (1911-13, rev. 1947)
   Pictures of pagan Russia in two parts by Igor Stravinsky and Nicolas Roerich
Édition Russe de Musique (S. et N. Koussewitzky)—Boosey and Hawkes
Paris, May 29, 1913, cond. Pierre Monteux

Renard (1916-17)
    A burlesque in song and dance
J. and W. Chester
Paris, June 3, 1922, cond. Ernest Ansermet

L'Histoire du soldat (The Soldier's Tale) (1918)
    To be read, played, and danced
J. and W. Chester
Lausanne, Sept. 28, 1918, cond. Ernest Ansermet

Pulcinella (1919)
    Ballet in one act. Music after themes, fragments, and pieces by G. B. Pergolesi
Édition Russe de Musique (S. et N. Koussewitzky)— Boosey and Hawkes
Paris, May 15, 1920, cond. Stravinsky

Suite for small orchestra (1924, rev. 1949)
Édition Russe de Musique (S. et N. Koussewitzky)— Boosey and Hawkes

Mavra (1922)
    Opera buffa in one act after Pushkin by Boris Kochno
Édition Russe de Musique (S. et N. Koussewitzky)— Boosey and Hawkes
Paris, June 3, 1922, cond. Gregory Fitelberg

Les Noces (The Wedding) (1923)
    Russian dance scenes with song and music
J. and W. Chester
Paris, June 13, 1923, cond. Ernest Ansermet

Oedipus Rex (1926-27, rev. 1948)
    Opera-oratorio in two acts for soloists, narrator, male chorus, and orchestra,
        after Sophocles, by Igor Stravinsky and Jean Cocteau
Édition Russe de Musique (S. et N. Koussewitzky)— Boosey and Hawkes
Paris, May 30, 1927, cond. Stravinsky

Apollon musagète (1927-28)
    Ballet in two scenes for string orchestra
Édition Russe de Musique (S. et N. Koussewitzky)— Boosey and Hawkes
Washington, D.C., April 27, 1928

Le Baiser de la fée (The Fairy's Kiss) (1928, rev. 1950)
  Allegorical ballet in four scenes
Paris, Nov. 27, 1928, cond. Stravinsky
  Divertimento (1938-39, rev. 1950)
  Suite for orchestra drawn from the ballet
Édition Russe de Musique (S. et N. Koussewitzky)— Boosey and Hawkes

Perséphone (1933-34)
  Melodrama in three parts by André Gide
  For tenor, mixed chorus, chorus of children, narrator
Édition Russe de Musique (S. et N. Koussewitzky)— Boosey and Hawkes
Paris, April 30, 1934, cond. Stravinsky

Jeu de cartes (Card Game) (1936)
  Ballet in three deals, choreographed by the author in
        collaboration with M. Malaieff
B. Schotts Söhne
New York, Apr. 27, 1937, cond. Stravinsky

Orpheus (1948)
  Ballet in three scenes
Boosey and Hawkes
New York, April 28, 1948, cond. Stravinsky

The Rake's Progress (1948-51)
  Opera in three acts. Libretto by W. H. Auden and Chester Kallman
Boosey and Hawkes
Venice, Sept. 11, 1951, cond. Stravinsky

Agon (1954-57)
  Ballet for twelve dancers
Boosey and Hawkes
Los Angeles, June 17, 1957, cond. Robert Craft

The Flood (1962)
  Biblical allegory based on Noah and the Ark
  For narrator, vocal soloists, chorus, orchestra, and dancers
Boosey and Hawkes
CBS television, June 14, 1962, cond. Stravinsky

Norton Books in Music

In the Norton Library

Norton / Haydn Society Records

MASTERPIECES OF MUSIC BEFORE 1750

Three 12-inch 33⅓ RPM Long-play records to supplement Parrish and Ohl, *Masterpieces of Music Before 1750.*

A TREASURY OF EARLY MUSIC

Four 12-inch 33⅓ RPM Long-play records to supplement Parrish, *A Treasury of Early Music.*